PERFECT PHRASES™

for

COMMUNICATING
CHANGE

**Hundreds of Ready-to-Use Phrases for
Maintaining Focus and Productivity During
Organizational Change**

Lawrence Polsky and Antoine Gerschel

Mc
Graw
Hill

New York   Chicago   San Francisco   Lisbon   London   Madrid   Mexico City
Milan   New Delhi   San Juan   Seoul   Singapore   Sydney   Toronto

The *McGraw·Hill* Companies

Copyright © 2010 by The McGraw-Hill Companies, Inc. All rights reserved. Printed in the United States of America. Except as permitted under the United States Copyright Act of 1976, no part of this publication may be reproduced or distributed in any form or by any means, or stored in a database or retrieval system, without the prior written permission of the publisher.

Trademarks: McGraw-Hill, the McGraw-Hill Publishing logo, Perfect Phrases, and related trade dress are trademarks or registered trademarks of The McGraw-Hill Companies and/or its affiliates in the United States and other countries and may not be used without written permission. All other trademarks are the property of their respective owners. The McGraw-Hill Companies is not associated with any product or vendor mentioned in this book.

1 2 3 4 5 6 7 8 9 10 11 12 13 14 15 16   WFR/WFR   1 9 8 7 6 5 4 3 2 1 0

ISBN 978-0-07-173831-6
MHID   0-07-173831-2

McGraw-Hill books are available at special quantity discounts to use as premiums and sales promotions or for use in corporate training programs. To contact a representative, please e-mail us at bulksales@mcgraw-hill.com.

Contents

Contents

Contents

Contents

Acknowledgments

This book would not exist without the amazing support, coaching, and encouragement of Anne Bruce. Anne's skill as an author, speaker, and coach is a role model we strive to follow.

Equally important is the positive guidance of our editors, Brian Foster, Julia Anderson Bauer, and Morgan Ertel. Brian's "you're doing fantastic, keep going" e-mails helped us many late nights when, as first-time authors, we wondered if we knew enough to fill the pages.

Thank you to our friends, family, and colleagues who cheered us on and gave us reality checks on our draft phrases to help them become perfect phrases.

To our customers who challenged us to help them communicate change in their organizations, where we learned what really works.

To the Tuscan Café in Warwick, New York, which provided food and sheltered us as we debated and laughed our way through the writing process. Thank you for saving our table!

Most important, to our wives, Noëmie and Teresa, who have been partners through our life changes and whom we have learned from and been inspired by in so many ways! And last but not least, to our kids Gretta, Giulia, Misha, Ron, and Zach, who go without us while we help change the world—this book is for you.

Chapter 1

Laying the Foundation for Communicating Change

The title of this book could be *How to Deliver—What May Be Initially Perceived as—Bad News*. Change at work is often hard to stomach. Employees tend to focus on what they are losing rather than the new opportunities change creates. We have written this book with that in mind and have tried to write the phrases in a way that makes them easy to hear during a stress-filled time.

In several sections, words and phrases are included that may be more empathic and soft than one might normally use. The purpose is not to force you to use those words, but to help you remember that such an approach may make employees more open to the content of what you're saying.

This also means you may not be able to use the phrases literally. For example, in some sections, there are lists of phrases that are choices. Pick the ones that match your style and situation. Then again, some of the phrases might need to be used and repeated, changing the emphasis each time.

During change, emotions run rampant, which clouds listening. People might only hear the downside of the message the first time, the next time they might hear more of the rationale, and the third time they might finally get "what's in it for me." Key messages need to be repeated over and over again. If you don't have the luxury of repeating something so many times, use active listening skills and ask back to find out how your message was received by the person you are talking to.

In addition to providing you with phrases to use, our intention is to offer some management training at the same time. Reviewing the content of phrases in any section also serves as a checklist, inspiration, and reminder to cover certain topics in your conversations. Rather than focus on just the words and whether they fit your style, focus on the content—the phrases will remind you what is important to discuss during the turbulent times you are leading people through.

In some sections, the phrases are ordered from most simple and nonconfrontational to more direct/more confrontational. At times "or" is used to signal you to choose the phrase that is most appropriate for you based on the situation/person you are talking to. For example, when communicating about job reassignment, there might be one phrase for a high performer and another for a low performer. The content in these phrases would be significantly different.

Moving from chapter to chapter, you'll notice that some of the phrases are the same or very similar. You will also notice that used in a different context they have a different feel and impact. In that spirit, look through several chapters before committing to a phrase to see if there is something similar that might work better for you.

Three Phases of Change: Change happens in three phases. First it must be launched, then it must be executed, and finally it must be sustained. In each phase, there are different critical communication challenges.

Launch Phase of Change

After all the hard work of deliberating and designing changes, the time for unveiling them to the organization has arrived. This usually begins with someone higher in the organization than you announcing what is being done. Maybe it is a downsizing or merger announced through the media. Perhaps an e-mail from the CEO or a division head informs you about a reorganization. An electronic town hall may be created with all employees in your division around the world to discuss the new enterprise resource planning (ERP) system that will change the way business is done.

Whatever the case may be, you have the responsibility to explain what the change means to your employees. Often you don't have all the information. Sometimes you don't have any information, and there is a good chance you are just as confused and uncertain as your team is.

There are several critical elements to address in the launch of any change—whether a reorganization, merger, new project, or new leader.

Explain the What and Why of Change

The what of change: People want to know what is happening. What is this new structure? Who is this new person? What is the new process? At launch, there is an insatiable need to know what is going on.

People also need to know what is *not* changing so they have some sense of stability within the storm. Even if you are implementing the most complex computer system, for example, some things will stay the same: company values, some of the people you work with, where your desk is, the customers you are servicing, or the products you are selling.

The why of change: More important, employees want to know why the change is being made. Why is it necessary to go through all this trouble? Why is it important to learn all these new things? Why do we have to change when things are going so well? Why this decision and not another? What is not working that needs fixing? What better future are we trying to create? Employees want to know why they are being asked to sacrifice and go through pain. That is the purpose of explaining the why. It gives people something to focus on and strive for while they are going through the challenges of change.

Remember, these are not children, nor is this an old-fashioned military operation. They will not just do something because you said so. In fact, research of United States Navy commanders shows that even those who simply say "just do it" and act dictatorially are less effective and efficient (Daniel Goleman, *Working with Emotional Intelligence*, 1998). Even in the armed forces they want to know why. People want the big picture. They need to know why.

Remember to include all the stakeholders in your what and why message. The best change launch messages include all of the people impacted. Knowing why the change is important for your customers, your colleagues, the other departments, the company, and the shareholders will give people a broader vision of what they are doing. It will help them understand the business context and keep them focused on key priorities.

Do It in Sixty Seconds or Less

Try it right now. Take sixty seconds and see if you can explain the what and the why of your change. How did it go? Traveling around the world, we have found that most leaders can't do it in sixty seconds. It is hard. It takes thought, preparation, and practice.

We call it the one-minute change message. It entails finding the essence of what is changing and why, and saying it in simple language. This is important for several reasons. First, employees today are swamped with communication: days booked with meetings; the constant ping of the BlackBerry; and innumerable chat messages popping up on their laptops. They are also pulled in many directions. The marketplace is volatile; priorities are constantly changing. You are lucky if you can get their attention for sixty seconds! When you have their attention, you want to make the best use of it. Sixty seconds may be all that you get.

Second, saying your message in one minute or less will force you to focus on key information. During change, there is so much information to share. Having a one-minute message will help employees weed through the information and hear what is really important.

Third, you are going to answer many questions and address many issues with employees. If you have to think through and create a response each time, you will never sound like you know what you are talking about.

Finally, change is filled with emotions. When people are emotional, their hearing gets clouded. They need to hear things over and over so that the message gets past the emotions and sinks in. When you have your prepared sixty-second change message in your back pocket, you are ready to provide employees with the key information they need to keep the big picture in mind.

Be Available to Talk to People

Leaders tell us one of the biggest challenges during change is dealing with all the employee questions, concerns, fears, and stress. Employees tell us that their biggest challenge during change is that they have all these questions, concerns, and fears and not enough access to leaders to get these addressed. This plays out often by leaders retreating to their offices to do e-mails and employees finding busywork to do rather than face the challenges of the change.

The tension of this situation is like a rubber band held between two fingers. The analogy works like this: There is a tension for the rubber band pulling in both directions. The employees on one side are pulling away because they want to run away and avoid the challenges. And the leaders on the other side are pulling away because they want to run away from all the employee issues. The only answer is for the leader side of the rubber band to move closer to the employee side.

Leaders need to talk, listen, and connect before employees get too stressed and the rubber band goes flying. This is the only way to dissipate the tension.

In order to talk, listen, and connect, you must find ways to be available. You are the voice and face of the company, like it or not. A major employee complaint we hear is that leaders are not available to discuss the changes. To respond, you must be available, perhaps by stopping by their cubes, putting an agenda item on your monthly staff meeting, or creating Web conferences. Find some way to simply check in regularly with employees, asking, "How are the changes going?" "What obstacles are you running into, and what can we do to remove them?" "What's the biggest fear out there this week?" Even asking "How are you?," can lead to a productive conversation. Take the time to listen and respond.

One last point: Many companies stop here. They spend a lot of energy and money launching the change. They fly around the world, create pretty posters and documents, and think they are done. This is wishful thinking. The main work of communicating change comes after the launch.

Execution Phase of Change

Now that the hard work of launching the change has occurred, the execution must begin. The execution phase is the longest and most challenging. It is filled not only with hard work but also with resistance. The main work of the execution phase involves performance management, handling resistance, and teamwork. Each of these areas has its own special needs. Below are our suggestions for handling each.

Performance Management

Two of the core challenges of executing change are that employees don't know what to do next or don't want to do what they know they need to do next. Good performance management addresses both challenges.

Clarifying Their Roles

Employees need to know what will be expected of them in the new environment. While this may seem obvious, we rarely see it done well. Much can be accomplished without spending a lot of time creating complicated job descriptions. There are four key questions to discuss:

- What will employees be doing?
- What will employees not be doing?
- Whom will employees be working with to get the job done?
- How will employees be measured?

In the "what employees will be doing" part of the conversation, discuss the main categories of work. This helps employees focus on their key priorities, which could be their involvement in a new project or an overview of their new roles. It does not need to include the detailed minutia of everyday responsibilities but rather can offer a broad overview. Often the details have not been worked out yet, and you cannot wait for those to be worked out to discuss the role. In the meantime, plow ahead, resolving to accept the ambiguity of the situation.

The "what employees will not be doing" discussion includes old responsibilities that no longer need to be done and anything that they will be passing off to a new person to handle. This part of the conversation prevents unnecessary work and conflicts. We have seen new computer systems rolled out but employees continued to produce and submit old reports for months because no one told them to stop! Also, with a change of structure or leadership, who does what may change. This can cause conflict between two people who both believe they are responsible for a task. Clarifying responsibilities upfront will go a long way to prevent conflict and lost time.

Within this discussion of roles, you need to clarify "who they will be working with to get the job done." This may be simple if they know and like their colleagues. It becomes more challenging when they don't like their new teammates, or when they are working with new people. Part of the challenge is the time it will take to get up to speed—they need to build new relationships in short order. Also, you need to help them break away from old relationship patterns while acknowledging that these old relationships are invaluable. This can all be accomplished through communication and coaching. Just don't underestimate the amount of time or energy it may take.

The final part of the discussion is about how employees will be measured. It is critical that these measures reinforce the goals of the change. Much of the anxiety about change revolves around not knowing how people will be viewed in the new world. Measures are a communication tool. They communicate to employees what is important. You can have the best one-minute change message explaining the what and why of change. However, if your measures are not consistent with that message, you are chasing your tail.

How will the new leader really notice employees' contributions to the team? Will their contributions in this new project be included in their annual reviews? Taking the time to explain this will relieve employees of the anxiety of the unknown, eliminate contradictions, and enable them to focus on their jobs. Additionally, you must make sure that their bonus system is in line with these measures. For example, we had a customer who was assigned the change of leading a new project that would take a significant amount of her time. However, her bonus was not adjusted accordingly. She was being paid on all her work *except* this project. It was no surprise she was apathetic and resentful toward the new project.

Articulate Short-Term Goals

Given the need to clarify employees' roles, a problem may exist in that often things are in such a state of flux even the leaders don't know the full plan and are unsure what to do first. Often they will wait, and wait, and wait, hoping that things get clearer or the need for the change passes. This, of course, is a recipe for stalled change.

Leaders need to set short-term goals. These goals may be daily, weekly, or monthly, but they help keep employees moving forward. As discussed earlier, mired in the confusion and emotion of the change, employees and leaders would just as soon put the work off. Setting simple daily or weekly goals makes the change manageable and keeps momentum going forward.

Creating Agreements

In clarifying roles, we frequently used the word *discuss*. The reason is simple. Telling people to do something is one thing. Getting them to agree to do it and be committed to doing it is quite another.

It is critical to get employee buy-in to the roles and goals. In the simplest case with a positive, functioning employee, this can done by simply asking, "What do you think about these _____ (goals/roles)?" Then listen to and respond to the comments. End the conversation by saying something like, "This is a team effort. I need your commitment that you will make these happen. I commit to you that I will support you. Can you give me your commitment?" For employees who are more resistant and have other issues, this may be a much longer discussion. See Chapter 6 for more assistance.

Responding to Mistakes/Fault Tolerance

With change comes learning. With learning come mistakes. Antoine's first boss was famous for saying, "Only those who don't work don't make mistakes!" This is especially true during change. We have to be willing to learn new skills, try new approaches, and so on. And that doesn't happen without a certain level of risk-taking. Companies and leaders who are willing to acknowledge, rather than punish, employees who make mistakes while trying something new tend to do better with change. Nothing does more to discourage change than blaming people for mistakes and finding scapegoats for whatever happens to go wrong.

Before talking to someone who has made a mistake, think about the impact your statement will have on that employee's willingness to take risks in the future.

Celebrating Success

Leaders in our Executing Change classes often struggle with how much positive reinforcement to give to their teams. They say, "Aren't people paid to do their job—why do I have to tell them they are doing it right?" "If they have been doing well for a long time, won't positive reinforcement seem patronizing?" "Don't we want to keep them trying to do even better?"

During high-stress situations, such as implementing change, when the pressure is on and results are critical, people need to know that they are on the right track and that their leaders are on their sides.

Find small things that are going right and tell your employees. Be specific. It will go a long way to support success during the stress of executing change. Don't worry about being too positive. We have never worked for or consulted with an organization where people have said, "We get too much positive reinforcement around here!"

Teamwork

Executing change successfully requires teamwork between leaders and employees and between employees. Change is easier to accomplish and less stressful when everyone is working together.

Getting Input from Team Members

During change, leaders often get stuck between wanting to involve employees and needing to make quick decisions. We have seen instances of under-involvement and over-involvement—each has its risks. When considering how much input to get for a new idea, process, or procedure, consider these questions:

- Do you have the technical knowledge to make a good decision? The less you know, the more you need to involve employees.
- How important is it that employees be committed to the solution? The more important this is, the more employee involvement is needed.
- What is the time line? The answers to the first two questions have to be tempered by the reality of the time line.

Communicating Common Goals and Shared Rewards

Organizations can't achieve change goals without leaders creating and explaining the specific team goals and team rewards accordingly. Employees need help translating change goals such "we want to become the market leader" into specific goals for their department, whether it is information technology or accounting. The CEO of a pharmaceutical company set a goal of "breaking down silos," but he never had the discipline to get his team (the function heads) together to share their goals and discuss overlaps and interdependencies. As a result, this goal was never achieved.

Resolving Conflicts

Hidden conflict is toxic during change. There are always real operational barriers to change. These barriers often overlap between people and responsibilities. It is critical to get these issues identified and discussed. The team leaders who encourage identification and discussion are the most successful. It can make a big difference to ask such simple questions as: "What do you think can sink this change?" "What do we have to change so that this change will work?"

The questions seem easy, but unless there is an environment of trust people will not share their observations and concerns. There is often fear of retribution for bringing up politically charged topics. But these are the most important topics to be addressed!

Cultivating Trust

All change comes with risk. You may be doing things for the first time and need help. Only in an environment where you can feel safe to be open and vulnerable will you seek out support. This ability to be vulnerable with colleagues is built on trust. Leaders foster this trust by

- doing what they say they are going to do,
- not criticizing employees in public,
- recognizing employees who take initiative, and
- thanking their teams for their contributions.

Sustain Phase of Change

There are three keys to executing change and getting employees focused on the future: listening to experience; acknowledging efforts, attitudes, and results; and articulating what's next.

Listening to Experience

As execution draws near the end, a key leadership task is for leaders to stop and listen to the experiences of their teams. By considering their input as to what worked well and what could be done better next time, organizations gain wisdom into making change succeed less painfully the next time—and there will be a next time.

Acknowledging Efforts, Attitudes, and Results

Good work deserves recognition. Taking the time to celebrate success will boost morale. Simple meetings, parties, luncheons, or financial rewards communicate to employees that their work did not go unappreciated. Such acknowledgments will help to secure employees' commitment for future change initiatives.

Articulating What's Next

A final task for leaders at the end of the change cycle is to set expectations for the future. This is a good time to discuss the next change initiatives coming down the road. Leaders need to also think through the business case for the need for continued adaptability and agility in order to succeed within the competitive landscape.

Balancing Information, Emotions, and Action

Within any change message, there are three distinct parts: the information or data to be shared, the emotion of the conversation, and the action that needs to be taken. These parts need to be carefully balanced to successfully support a change initiative.

Information

People need information during change—the hard, cold facts. This information might include the details of the new procedures, processes, and plans as well as who will be doing what and when. These pieces form the core of any message and are the easiest to communicate. But before actually communicating the information, consider the emotions involved in the message.

Emotions

There is one thing that is guaranteed during any change—emotions will be flying! The fear, frustration, and anxiety that come with any change cloud the retention of information. It is all too common that critical data get forgotten and key requirements are misunderstood. While it may feel like a conspiracy, it is not! It is the emotions of change at play.

Overcommunicate

Our rule during change is to communicate seven to ten times more than you normally would. In all our years in this work, we have seen only one organization border on overcommunicating about change. It announced the closing and relocating of a base of operations three years in advance and had countless meetings, booklets, and publications available about the change. It recognized this was an emotional change and there was no shortage or perceived shortage of information.

Everywhere else we have observed, leaders seem to think that if they have told employees twice about a change, it is enough. But we have found that, given all the emotions involved, employees need to hear the change-related messages over and over.

Think about when you have changed jobs, either by choice or mandate. How many times did you have to go to your manager to get clarification on duties, decisions, resources, procedures, processes, contacts, and so on? Probably a lot! That is because the situation was new. When a situation is new, you are learning. While learning, people are often stressed out from such emotions as confusion and wanting to make a good impression.

Check on Your Team's Emotions

As a leader, you want to do what you can to help your people through the emotions of change. At the same time it can be difficult to read their emotions. Your own emotions and how you expect them to react will cloud your judgment.

Helping your employees move through emotions involves two steps: assessing and taking action. The problem we often see is that leaders take action before assessing how employees are doing. The solution is perception checking.

Perception checking means saying something like: "You seem a little (fill in the emotion you are observing such as stressed, scared, confused, upset, etc), is that right?" This will give your employee the chance to clarify (or not) your perception. If you are right, he or she might give you some more information as to why. If you are wrong, you will be informed as to what is really going on. Either way, you will know what your employee is feeling. From there, you can work together to support the employee's success.

Address Emotions Directly in Discussions
One way to dissipate emotions and reduce their behind-the-scenes impact during change is to identify and discuss them. For example, if your employees are anxious about the change in a new process and the impact on their workloads, say something like, "I know many of you are anxious about the changes and the impact on our workloads. Let's take a few minutes to discuss it." Employees are looking for a place to discuss their feelings. This discussion will either happen with you or with their friends through instant messaging or over lunch. If you create a forum to express emotions, it will not only help employees move through them, but it will give you much needed information as to what is really going on. Otherwise, the important information about fears and issues will not be shared with you, and you will be leading with one eye closed.

Action

Information may be available abundantly and emotions handled well, but that does not guarantee progress. In fact, information overload or too much satisfaction at work can lead to stagnation and paralysis! Include action statements in change messages. Phrases such as "the next step is" and "I expect you to" will help keep progress moving. They will also provide a means to test whether your audience has gotten the change message. People can easily hide behind nice words and trying to please you verbally. Taking action is the only way to show that the change message was received.

For example, the organization mentioned earlier that did such a great job of communicating about change slipped up in taking action. Because there was so much time for people to decide if they were going to relocate or not, there was inaction. Employees were waiting for various reasons. Some were waiting to see if they could get better offers; some were waiting because they were indecisive; and others were waiting because they thought the leaders would change their minds and not relocate! Whatever the case, this created an extra burden of stress and lack of productivity while everyone was waiting around.

Three Common Mistakes Leaders Make When Communicating Change

We have seen leaders fail in communicating change in three basic ways: not telling enough, not listening enough, and not telling the truth enough.

Not Telling Enough

Leaders are usually ahead of the people they are leading. They usually know information before employees and have thought through situations before employees even know what is going on. This can lead them to forget that employees do not know what they know. The result is many leaders do not communicate enough. Not only is it important to share information, it is important to repeat it often. When stressed, scared, or overwhelmed, people need to hear things many times before it sinks in.

Not Listening Enough

As in other areas in life, leaders' default communication mode during change is telling, not listening. Some reasons for this are:

- The chaos and ambiguity of change drive leaders to think they need to have all the answers. They feel obliged to lead, which often translates as give direction. Then, they focus their time

on trying to give employees all the answers rather than have dialogues.
- Telling people what to do is easier than asking them how things are going and then really listening to the answer.

If leaders do ask questions, they tend to avoid the most important or tough ones. Leaders might not have dealt with or assimilated the reality of the changes yet and are uncomfortable asking employees about the same topics. This leaves employees feeling like leaders do not really care about what they think. Some good questions to ask are: "What do you think can really kill this change?" "What do you need to make this work?" These are the topics that employees want to talk about and leaders often do not want—but need—to address.

Not Telling the Truth Enough

As Dr. Robert Schachat, a veteran executive coach and one of our mentors, used to tell his clients and friends alike about honest feedback, "Give it to me, I can take it!" One constant leadership dilemma during change is the issue of how much truth employees can take. On the one hand, leaders want to be open and disclose what they can. However, there is fear that since emotions are running high, too much information or the "wrong" information will distract or upset employees. The problem emerges when the pressure to succeed pushes up against the need to know. In our experience, we have found that employees can take the truth yet leaders hold it back. Our advice: Give it to them—they can take it.

Communicating Change Virtually

Today's organizational changes involve employees spread around regions, countries, and continents. Virtual tools like GoToWebinar, Skype, blogs, and Facebook offer a terrific amount of added flexibility to communicate with people. Yet, there are also many limitations and challenges when communicating change in this new digital world.

In principal, all the rules of communicating change apply in virtual situations. In fact, they are amplified because when you are not face-to-face, it is more critical to follow all of the guidelines. For example, overempathize in emotional situations that are virtual since there are no facial expressions to be read by the speaker. Similarly, it is important to increase the frequency of communication, since out of sight can lead to out of mind. Be crystal clear about the business case for change so you can communicate it succinctly over the phone or in short e-mails.

A main challenge for leaders is choosing the best media for messages. Often time and money are limited, making face-to-face communication a luxury. Yet, change is emotional and usually requires personal connections to gain employee commitment and buy-in. We have found that there is no perfect answer—it is usually a gray zone.

Within the gray zone there are two extreme ends. At one end are the one-dimensional media: e-mails, chats, and blogs. At the other end of the continuum is multidimensional communication, the epitome of which is face-to-face conversation. Toward the middle of the continuum are multidimensional media such as phone conversations, Web meetings, and video-conferencing. When deciding which media to use to communicate change, there are eight dimensions to consider.

1. **Transactional vs. relationship.** Is the interaction a series of single steps with little human component, or does it include significant interpersonal dynamics or goals?
2. **Facts vs. emotions.** Is the purpose of the dialogue to share "dry" facts, or does it include emotional topics?
3. **Information sharing vs. collaborating.** Is the communication simply exchanging information with a person, or is the goal to work closely together to solve a problem?

4. **Repetition vs. innovation.** Are you involved in a task that you have done before with success, or are you exploring new territory?

5. **Maintaining relationship vs. relationship issue.** Is everything going well in an existing relationship, or are tensions and conflict looming?

6. **Structured vs. unstructured.** Are there perfectly clear roles, responsibilities, or milestones, or are you trying to figure out what needs to be done and who should do it?

7. **Simplicity vs. complexity.** Is the message to be communicated simple and straightforward, or will it require thinking and discussion?

8. **Audience similarities vs. audience disparities.** Do they speak the same language? Do they know you? What are their skill levels and experience with the content of the message? What are their cultural or social conventions?

The following sections describe different reasons for communicating and what media work best.

Announcing Change

Organizational, high-level change information is transactional. Often it involves simply getting the facts out. This can be done through a simple e-mail if the content is not complex, is not a pep talk, and does not contain major underlying emotional issues. To get individual buy-in and commitment when announcing change, focus more on the relationships of individuals with their managers and the company. This makes the message as much emotional as factual, and it requires at least a multidimensional medium, such as a Web conference.

Responding to Questions

When responding to technical questions, FAQ sheets, e-mail technical support, or phone support work well. But when there are personal or emotional questions, such as job fit, role conflict, or career questions, multidimensional communication methods (i.e., face-to-face meetings) are recommended.

Creating Urgency

Urgency can be generated through a simple e-mail. For example, setting a deadline and copying the other person's boss can create urgency. Sending a note about a high value bonus as an incentive to get something done also can create urgency. But don't forget the relationship and emotional aspects of communication. If you want to manage the emotional reactions of others, use e-mail cautiously.

Clarifying Roles and Responsibilities

The first round of reviewing new roles and making final clarifications can be done through e-mail. E-mail can also work very well to increase comprehension when the corporate language is different than the regional language. In cases when there are strong emotional reactions, power struggles, or loss of influence due to job changes, e-mail will not work.

Communicating Individual Objectives

E-mails can start the discussion of individual objectives, but a key aspect of setting objectives is mutual agreement. This usually requires a personal discussion to create a common understanding and a stronger personal commitment.

Empowering Employees

After you have created an environment of empowerment that works, you can use e-mail to delegate assignments. If you need to ensure employees have a clear understanding of the expectations and boundaries of their empowerment, use a multidimensional media.

Keeping People Motivated

Reminders and congratulations are well suited to e-mail. This creates a formal record. In cases where the issue is important or an employee went well above and beyond, making a phone call or face-to-face visit gives an extra impact.

Complaints about a leader, interpersonal conflicts between key stakeholders, or challenges integrating changes in another country are all instances when emotions can run high and an e-mail or phone call won't do. Part of being a leader is recognizing these situations and taking the time, energy, and money to have a face-to-face interaction. Sometimes you just need to get on a plane!

Best Practices

While there are no magic words that fit every situation, there are some best practices we have discovered over the years.

- **Build trust before change.** The time to start building trusting relationships is before you need them! In times of change, the trust between you and your people is critical. If you don't have trust, it may be too late to have real communication. Employees who trust you will hear the perfect phrases as you intend them. This will create meaningful dialogue. However, if your relationship with them is damaged from past errors, employees may hear any phrase as more "B.S." from management.

- **Be direct.** We have found that many leaders either avoid difficult topics or are too timid with their people in tough change situations. For this reason, you will find many of the phrases in Chapter 6, "Perfect Phrases for Handling Resistance," are direct and firm. It is often most effective to just give it to them straight rather than tiptoe around tough situations. Employees respect this. It tells employees you can be relied on for the truth. Also, in these days of corporate executive deceit, leaders have to go the extra mile to prove they are not one of the crooked lot.

- **Talk to key people early.** In the absence of information, people make up stories. The faster you discuss news—even bad news—the less negativity is created. With delays come rumors and false expectations. Get the news out as fast as you can. It will not only reduce anxiety, but it will give your team the time to start moving through a process that is often longer than you can predict.

- **Adjust to your audience.** While leaders may think they are just "sending" a change message, there is always someone having a reaction. Don't forget to adapt your message to this reaction. Look at those you are speaking with and notice how they respond and react. Pay attention to what their facial expressions, body language, tone of voice, or e-mail word choices are. Some of the executives we work with undermine themselves because they overlook those signals. They are either too much in a rush to get the message out or overly involved with their own anxieties when delivering the news. Remember to adapt your message to your audience because whenever you are communicating change it is a two-way process.

- **Watch your body language**. Most leaders know the adage: It's not what you say but how you say it. But it is worth repeating here. You have to believe in what you're saying. If you don't, your body language will give you away and no one will believe you. During times of change, employees are looking for the truth. You will need to find ways to tell the truth in a way that is believable.

- **Find your style**. Don't get hung up on picking the perfect word; rather, find a style that works for your personality. Each leader has his or her own style. Some have a flair for the dramatic. Others focus on being inspiring. Some speak plainly and directly. They can all be equally effective change communicators. The same is true of the phrases in this book. Depending on where you stand, our phrases may be too cutthroat or too nice, too cheesy or too formal. Find the style and words that fit your personality and situation.

- **Choose the right person to deliver the message.** Who delivers the message makes an impression. For example, when communicating about a new position title—whether the message comes from a high-level executive or a Human Resources person has a very different effect. Having a senior business leader who you report to will have a big positive impact. However, choosing the leader closest to the employee may also be a good idea because that leader is trusted more and can better tailor the message to the audience. There is no simple formula. Choose the person who will create the best result.

- **Don't expect to have all the answers.** You won't and can't have all the answers to questions you're going to be asked during change. It is a characteristic of change that a lot of details are clarified as the change implementation makes progress. Yet, employees continuously search for security and clarity. In such cases it is best to just say, "I'll find it for you" and then find out. If there is no answer, tell them so and leverage the phrases in this book to help them understand why. Remember, questions are a great opportunity to reinforce your business case for change.

- **Don't expect the "perfect phrase."** You prepare and plan. Then you get in the room and the human being(s) opposite you have a reaction different from what you expected. This is life. You will need to continually adjust your words, tone, and focus to get your message across. Rest assured that the best spontaneous conversations are well planned. Thinking through and practicing your words will definitely help you get as close to perfect as humanly possible!

Easy-to-Use Checklist for Change Messages

This checklist can be used while creating a change message. It is intended to help you ensure you create the highest-impact message possible. Remember to craft a message you can deliver in sixty seconds or less.

- ❑ What kind of change is it?
  - ❑ New structure (i.e., reorganization, layoffs, outsourcing, merger, new teams)
  - ❑ New project (i.e., ERP/software rollout, process improvement, innovation)
  - ❑ New leader (i.e., succession, merger/acquisition, new team member)
  - ❑ New strategy (i.e., new markets, new positioning, new products/services)
- ❑ What is the nature of the message?
  - ❑ Announcing change
    - ❑ Identify what is changing and what is not
    - ❑ Get clear on why the change is important to the business/team/customer/employees

- ❑ Responding to questions
  - ❑ List the questions you expect and check your answers for accuracy
  - ❑ Determine who else can provide you with critical information
- ❑ Overcoming fear
  - ❑ Identify, by employee or employee group, what they are most scared of
  - ❑ See the fear from their point of view
  - ❑ Decide how you will you reassure them
- ❑ Coaching
  - ❑ For skill
  - ❑ For emotions
  - ❑ For flexibility
  - ❑ Empathize
  - ❑ Identify current behavior
  - ❑ Set expectations
  - ❑ Support success
- ❑ Dealing with performance problems
  - ❑ Clarify the performance agreement
  - ❑ Identify current behavior
  - ❑ Define the impact on change success
  - ❑ Set expectations for the future
  - ❑ Plan responses for expected employee defensiveness and reactions
  - ❑ Get commitment
- ❑ Handling resistance
  - ❑ Empathize
  - ❑ Level with them
  - ❑ Remember to listen
  - ❑ Take a stand

- ❏ Rallying team
    - ❏ Identify members that need rallying
    - ❏ Locate past experiences of success they can relate to
    - ❏ Clarify goals, roles, and standards
    - ❏ Celebrate success
    - ❏ Recognize people
    - ❏ Optimize work processes
- ❏ Prepare for delivering your message by thinking through:
    - ❏ How well the audience knows you
    - ❏ How well they know the subject matter
    - ❏ What is in it for them to listen and take action
    - ❏ What other priorities or issues may distract them from hearing you
    - ❏ Who needs to be consulted or copied before sending a communication
    - ❏ How to ensure the message is heard as intended
    - ❏ How the message will impact the motivation level of employees
    - ❏ Whether the message has the right balance of information, emotion, and call to action
    - ❏ Other documentation needed to supplement the message

Chapter 2

Perfect Phrases for Communicating a New Organizational Structure

New structures are the most complex of organizational changes. They can involve many levels of change: changes in responsibilities and roles, a new supervisor and/or new teammates, new customers, new performance metrics, a new compensation plan, and—potentially the most disruptive of all changes—layoffs. We have provided phrases to handle a wide range of potential situations. Remember to review them and find the words and style that work best for your particular situation.

Announcing Change

New Structure Business Case

The new structure is _____.

We are implementing this new structure to:

> *respond to our global customer base.*
> *adapt to changing economic conditions.*

uphold industry best practices.

create a more entrepreneurial environment.

attract the best and the brightest.

save money.

New Manager

You are now reporting to _____ .

The reason this is changing is because:

she is known as an expert in the field.

she is a terrific mentor.

she is trusted by the executives.

she knows this process inside and out.

she is on a developmental assignment.

we want you to learn everything you can from her for your next assignment.

she was selected by the committee as the best choice to replace _____ , based on her background.

What questions do you have?

You may need to add:

I know you were hoping to get this job. We looked closely at you as a candidate. You have some great experience. We appreciate your contributions to the company. However, we don't think you are ready for this position yet. We think you need to _____ to prepare for this kind of position. There will be other opportunities for you to advance in the company.

Or

I know you were hoping to get this job. We looked closely at you as a candidate. We felt you were not as qualified for this position because:

*you did not meet some critical deadlines in the past, such as
when _____.*

*your performance in the last performance review cycle
dropped.*

*you still need to work on your technical skills, such
as _____.*

*you are not willing to relocate, which may happen with this
position.*

*this position requires a greater percentage of travel time than
you are able to commit to.*

What questions do you have?

New Peers

**You will now be working closely with _____ as a peer,
who is in charge of _____.**

**I know that you used to be the sole individual responsible
for _____. This new structure may seem like it will be
more time-consuming/more difficult/less efficient. However, the
reason for this structural change is to:**

improve our response time to the customer.

bring critical decisions closer to the work team.

make decisions faster.

*break down silos so that we can come up with new ideas that
incorporate points of view from key individuals across
divisions.*

increase information-sharing across divisions.

*increase our exposure to other points of view before
implementing decisions.*

*provide you with more time, which will help you increase both
your output and leverage and enable you to keep pace with
the greater number of projects you will be taking on.*

What questions do you have?

You may need to add:

I know you used to work on these projects jointly with
_____ *. You have performed well together in the past,*
have gotten to know each other, and know how to be productive
together. Now you will be working with _____,
even if you think _____ *has more know-how. Your*
new assignment doesn't mean you should not stay connected
with _____ *, as the two of you have forged a valuable*
relationship.

New Title
Your title will be changing to _____ *. This means you*
will be reporting to _____ *and are now responsible*
for _____ *. Your new team will be comprised of the*
following individuals: _____ *.*

We have assigned you to this new responsibility because:

> *of your past contributions.*
>
> *of your experience in similar situations/industries/projects/*
> *regions.*
>
> *of feedback we have received from* _____ *.*
>
> *we need someone in this position that we/our employees/our*
> *customers trust.*
>
> *we need someone in this position who can quickly adapt to the*
> *changing company/economic environment.*
>
> *you have a very good relationship with* _____ *, who*
> *is a key partner/customer/supplier of this company.*
>
> *we want to provide you with a developmental opportunity to*
> *gain important experience regarding* _____ *.*

What questions do you have?

Congratulations! Welcome to the new team!

You may need to add:

> *This may not be exactly what you were expecting or hoping for. Nevertheless, your new assignment is an opportunity to broaden your experience in _____. It also will help you in the future as we continue to _____. We value you as a contributor and are counting on you to fulfill the responsibilities of this job.*

For best practices, make sure you don't make commitments about possible future opportunities to resolve short-term concerns with the situation. Doing so will only raise employee expectations and create more problems down the road.

New Compensation Model
We are introducing a new compensation/bonus program. This new compensation model was developed in response to changes in our new structure, such as:

> *our new customer coverage area.*
>
> *new team member responsibilities.*
>
> *increased/decreased employee workload.*
>
> *our new quality targets.*
>
> *our recent regional expansion.*
>
> *your supervision of a larger group of direct reports.*
>
> *our new global approach to conducting business, which necessitates a global compensation model.*
>
> *the need to align/harmonize disparate compensation models within the organization.*

> *I have distributed an information package that details the components of the new compensation model.*

Please read the information package, which includes very practical examples to help you understand how the new compensation model impacts your pay.

Feel free to approach your Human Resources representative or me with your questions.

If the new compensation model involves the reduction of 401(k)/other benefits/hours for hourly employees, you may need to add:

Unfortunately we have to reduce our expenses. We have decided to save the jobs of all of our employees and instead reduce 401(k) contributions/other benefits/individual weekly hours.

As you know, the economic climate has changed dramatically and our customers have been spending less. The poor economic conditions have greatly impacted our results. We have no choice but to implement a new compensation model that will reduce our 401(k) contributions/other benefits/individual weekly hours in order to cut back our costs.

The good news is:

> *the company is still contributing to your 401(k).*
>
> *as an employee of this company, you are provided with some very valuable benefits, such as _____ .*
>
> *our total compensation package compares favorably with packages of other companies in the industry/our competitors/other companies in the region.*

For hourly workers who are worried about cutbacks to their hours, you may need to add:

I have tried to accommodate your needs as much as possible and have assigned you to your favorite time slots. However, as of now, you will not be allowed to work as many hours on _____ .

I know this is not good news, but we have no choice except to make cutbacks to our employees' weekly hours. Do you have questions?

I don't want to miss the opportunity to remind you that you are a very important member of the team! I value your work and contributions. We are doing everything we can to turn things around.

For best practices make sure you

- understand and have all the information;
- have all the answers and details employees will ask for *before* having a conversation with them about the new compensation package;
- give them the information and then listen and empathize; and
- give them ample time to process the information.

Layoffs
As part of this restructuring, unfortunately, we have no choice but to reduce the workforce by _____ .

One of the toughest aspects of any manager's job is laying off valued collaborators. We are not taking this restructuring lightly and will follow up with more information as soon as it is available.

Be assured that we will honor all of our obligations to our employees and will make it our utmost priority to transition through this layoff as smoothly as possible.

We are restructuring our company to adapt to changing market conditions and to build our strength for the future. We want/ need to:

> *better serve our global customers by implementing key global account management.*

eliminate redundant positions from the merger.

eliminate noncore functions.

align our employee headcount with our new business processes.

be able to leverage talent from other sources.

lower our expenses.

Despite the challenges we currently are facing, we are very confident that this restructuring will position us to _____ (reiterate vision and positive outlook). We feel this way because:

our market share is growing by _____ .

our _____ solutions/technology are cutting-edge.

we have a very loyal customer base.

our employees are the most talented _____ in the industry.

we have a very strong balance sheet and secure financial backing.

we have very balanced product and solutions portfolios that reach across industries and regions.

For best practices, make sure you

- understand and have all the information;
- don't argue with your employees or defend the layoff as you risk minimizing its impact and inflaming emotions;
- give them ample time to process the information; and
- don't say there will be no more layoffs unless you are 100 percent sure of it!

In cases when you aren't sure whether or not more layoffs may be coming, focus on the challenges that you know lie ahead as well as on the strength of the new structure and the company/team.

Changes to Customer/Supplier/Partner Assignments
Going forward, you will be taking care of _____ . We are making this change because:

> you have experience with this customer/supplier/partner/ industry/region.
>
> you have succeeded in the past with demanding customers/ suppliers/partners.
>
> we see this as a developmental opportunity that will give you important experience regarding _____ .

What questions do you have?

Responding to Questions

Why Didn't We Create a _____ Structure Instead?
We are implementing this new structure to:

> respond to our global customer base.
>
> adapt to changing economic conditions.
>
> uphold industry best practices.
>
> create a more entrepreneurial environment.
>
> attract the best and the brightest.
>
> save money.

Based on these objectives, we considered several structural options, including _____ .

We selected the new structure because it will enable us to:

> be number one in the market by _____ .
>
> grow by _____ .
>
> diversify by adding _____ .
>
> expand into _____ .
>
> reduce our response time to _____ .

improve our operating margins.

reduce our costs.

take our time to implement it.

find ways to best leverage our current expertise, rather than hire new people.

maintain our company culture.

Or

Given the situation, we had no choice but to implement this new structure because _____ .

How Will We Serve Our Customers During the Transition?
Serving our customers is at the core of our business and the lifeblood of our company. This structural change should not interfere with our dedication to providing the highest level of customer service.

If you are aware of a situation in which our change activities are interfering with our customer service, please ask your manager for assistance.

We are in the process of working on relevant communications to our customers. We will be distributing a template to assist you by _____ .

Will There Be Layoffs?
This is a very good question. I appreciate your raising it. We have carefully evaluated the situation and came to the conclusion that there will be no layoffs. Everyone will be offered a job.

Or

This is a very good question. I appreciate your raising it. We have carefully evaluated the impact of this decision

*on our organization and believe that if everything goes
according to plan, there will be no layoffs. However, if _____
doesn't go as planned, we may have to _____. We
say this in the spirit of full disclosure. In the meantime, let me
assure you that the probability of this happening is minimal
because _____. Last but not least, I would like to
emphasize that this new strategy does not have staff reduction
as part of its objectives. It is being done to meet the objectives
outlined above.*

Or

*This is a very good question. I appreciate your raising it. It is
possible that this new structure will have an impact on our
headcount. We don't know what we don't know. Currently, I
can assure you that, for the short-term, no layoffs have been
decided.*

For best practices in case of looming job losses, define a talent-
retention strategy for key contributors you don't want to lose.

Be prepared to answer questions such as:

- Who was involved in the decision to restructure the company?
- What is the competition doing?
- How much will this cost?
- How will we know if this is working?

Overcoming Fear

High Performers Scared of Losing Their Jobs
*I understand your concern. You are a key contributor, and I will
do all that I can to keep you at this company. Expect to hear
from me by _____ with:*

> *more information.*
> *a formal offer.*
> *a new job description.*

Middle Performers Scared of Losing Their Jobs

Based on my experience in similar situations, I agree that your concerns about staff reductions are legitimate. I am not expecting that anyone will be laid off, but it never hurts to update your résumé and keep in touch with your network.

Don't forget that there are plenty of potential opportunities for you to explore and connect to the network that exists within our company.

Just relax and see what happens. I have found that once the dust settles from a company restructuring, there often are plenty of opportunities for employees to tackle new challenges and experiences.

Low Performers Scared of Losing Their Jobs

I understand your concerns, and to be frank, there is a possibility that some people may lose their jobs. Although I cannot say at this time that it is 100 percent certain, given the current circumstances, I suggest you update your résumé and reactivate your network.

Of course, the company restructuring may not affect our division. But it never hurts to update your résumé and reactivate your network.

High Performers Worried About Having the Right Skills

I understand you are concerned that you do not have the skill set needed right now. You are not alone. Most of us will be learning as we go along.

Tell me what you are struggling with and what you think you need to succeed.

We will make sure that you get the appropriate coaching/ mentoring/training to succeed.

Middle Performers Worried About Having the Right Skills
This new environment may in fact be a bit of a stretch for you.

Please tell me what areas are challenging for you.

Let's see how this new structure unfolds. Be sure to keep in touch with me about how you are adapting to the restructuring. I will do my best to find people and resources to support you.

Low Performers Worried About Having the Right Skills
I understand your concerns. We will have to evaluate your future options very carefully. Let's schedule a meeting with your Human Resources representative to discuss:

> *other possible positions within the company that might better suit you.*

> *what support we can offer you should you decide to transition out of the company.*

Employees Worried About Getting Along with New People
Your concerns are valid. We will have to carefully configure our new team.

In order to ease the company's transition into our new structure, we plan to offer:

> *team-building activities.*

> *formal and informal meetings.*

> *language and culture briefings.*

> *virtual communication training.*

> *updated job profiles to all team members.*

What else can I do to support the new team's success?

If someone senses that there may be potential problems with incorporating new employees into the restructured company, you may need to add:

> *I understand why you are worried. Getting to know and work with some of these new colleagues may not be so easy. However, we are laying a framework to support the transition. For example, we are _____.*

> *What else can I do to support the new team's success?*

Or if someone knows that he has a specific problem with another employee, you may need to add:

> *I know that you and _____ have had some problems working together in the past. You two need to get together and figure out how to improve your working relationship. This collaboration is very important to the team/department because _____.*

> *What do you think I can do to support your success?*

> *If necessary, your Human Resources representative or I may be able to step in and help resolve your issues with _____.*

Creating Urgency

Keeping the Momentum
It is critical that we implement this new structure now so that we can:

> *stay number one in the market.*
> *become number one in the market by _____.*
> *grow our business by _____.*
> *diversify by adding _____.*

expand into _____ .

reduce our response time to _____ .

improve our operating margins.

comply with (new) legal requirements.

By doing so, you/our team will be able to:

increase your/their salary/bonus.

save your/their job(s).

create more career opportunities.

improve work/life balance.

learn new skills.

have the opportunity to work with new regions/customers.

Addressing Power Struggles and Career Issues

Someone Scared of Losing Power/Influence

I know that this may look like a demotion or a loss of influence, but please consider that:

you are gaining new functional/regional responsibilities.

you are now in a position that provides you with the work/life balance you have been looking for/more free time/less stress.

you are now closer to research/operations/legal/projects and have fewer administrative responsibilities.

you will be making as much as/more than you were in your previous position.

you will be in charge of a team that is as large as/larger than your previous team.

you will be the final decision maker on _____ .

you will be a key contributor to _____ .

*you will be working closely with _____ , who is a
leading expert/major player/recognized personality in the
field.*

*your new responsibilities will position you for future
_____ .*

Your new position is important because you will be:

managing the largest division in our department.

bringing in the biggest margin to the company.

in charge of key customers.

heading up the largest growth market.

involved in a new strategic area within the company.

supported by state-of-the-art technology/research.

**You have played a key role in our success. We recognize that.
We're counting on you to continue to contribute as you have in
the past.**

How Does This Influence Career Opportunities?
This restructuring may impact your career opportunities.

Let's discuss your current career objectives. What are they?

**Try not to overreact. Once the dust settles, new opportunities will
arise. We just need to finalize a few outstanding factors first.**

**Let's keep our eyes open to all possible options. There may be
opportunities to move up in the company, but you might also
consider making a lateral move to gain experience in other
functions/industries/divisions.**

**I am committed to your success and will help you navigate
through the organization when new opportunities arise.**

If someone is no longer sure how he or she fits into the organization,
you may need to add:

This is a big change, but it also may serve as an opportunity for you to reevaluate your options. Let's observe how the restructuring evolves. If you reach the point where you think that you no longer fit into this company, I would be happy to support your transition to a new company.

If someone no longer fits into the organization, you may need to add:

I think it would make sense for us to schedule a meeting with our Human Resources representative to discuss your options.

For best practices, talk to your HR representative to discuss options *before* talking to an employee who is no longer a good fit.

Clarifying Roles and Responsibilities

Let's talk about your new role. I have captured the key elements of your new position on this one sheet of paper, which includes:

your title.

the name of your supervisor.

key performance measures.

the names of your team members.

your main responsibilities.

Also, let's discuss how your new position differs from what you have been doing until now:

You will continue to _____ because _____ .

You will also now be responsible for _____ because _____ .

You will no longer be responsible for _____ because _____ .

You also will be sharing some of your responsibilities with _____ . He/she will become a key partner of yours. We will define individual contributions, coordination needs, work evaluations, and so on, as we move along with each of the projects/tasks.

What questions do you have?

What are your thoughts about this?

How does this compare with what you expected/what you were hoping for?

As a first step to get you oriented to your new role, I'd like you to interview our main business partners in other departments to discover what business problems and objectives are driving their work.

Communicating Individual Objectives

Clarifying What Is Expected

For the purposes of this discussion, please refer back to the change announcement and its accompanying communication document, which reiterates the overall objectives of the new structure. To refresh your memory, those objectives are _____ .

Our team is a key contributor to the rapid and successful implementation of the new structure. We have talked about your new role and its accompanying responsibilities.

With company changes like this, there is a risk that individual objectives will get lost in the commotion, which makes it even more important for us to stay focused as we implement the new structure.

Let's focus on your initial/short-term goals. Within the next three weeks, I'd like you to:

> *contact your new counterparts in _____ and introduce yourself.*
>
> *have a staff meeting to review the changes with your team and answer any questions.*
>
> *set goals with your direct reports.*
>
> *analyze the budget and its implications for the next quarter.*
>
> *contact all of your customers and set up meetings to review our new _____ .*
>
> *have one-on-one conversations with each of your team members about their new roles.*

Empowering Employees

Individual Contributors

We have communicated the what and the why of the new structure and have made all the necessary high-level decisions. We now need you to bring the new structure to life by:

> *learning the company's policies and procedures without hiding behind them. You are your own boss within the parameters of our policies and new structure.*
>
> *being crystal clear about what you want to achieve in your new position. Put your goals and responsibilities in writing. Never set or accept goals/objectives that do not have specific measures. Share your goals with me/your peers/ your direct reports. Doing so will help us all take ownership of the new structure and stay focused.*
>
> *making a list of assumptions, constraints, resources, and other givens. Then challenge the validity of each.*

focusing on what you can *achieve and influence. Don't get discouraged by things you can't control.*

recognizing and changing counterproductive thinking patterns, such as apathy, defiance, and playing the victim.

learning how to handle requests that are beyond your resources or capabilities by giving alternative options and saying no in a professional manner.

speaking up if you have a question or don't agree with a business decision. You may be right.

learning about the key z (financial, operational, sales, etc.) we are using to track our performance. Ask somebody in accounting, a peer, or your manager to help you analyze these indicators.

taking a course in business finance, business acumen, or operations to help you make decisions in the larger context of our new structure.

Leaders
We have communicated the what and the why of the new structure and have made all the necessary high-level decisions. We now need you to bring the new structure to life by:

looking at your new business/division/region/department/ team and further fleshing out how it is affected by the new structure.

thinking about how the higher level, overall objectives of the new structure apply to your business/division/region/ department/team. Make sure you define individual objectives accordingly.

reviewing your resources and seeing how you can reallocate them to accommodate the new structure.

> *involving your direct reports, and within reason delegating as much of the communication and implementation tasks to them as possible.*
>
> *regularly reviewing your own and your department's progress with implementing the new structure.*
>
> *keeping me and other key stakeholders informed of your commitments and your progression in implementing the new structure.*
>
> *making sure you clarify job descriptions with your team. They need to know what is expected of them. Refer to their job descriptions to understand, and where necessary, clarify their roles and responsibilities.*
>
> *involving all stakeholders as early as possible.*
>
> *learning/applying techniques that will facilitate effective brainstorming sessions.*
>
> *seeking to break complex situations into smaller, easier to manage components.*

Keeping People Motivated

By Providing Clarity of Vision/Direction

The vision of the new structure is to _____ .

Based on your new responsibilities:

> *the goals for next week are _____ .*
>
> *your number one priority is _____ .*
>
> *your most important customer is _____ .*
>
> *the most important criterion for success is _____ .*
>
> *your key performance measure is _____ .*
>
> *don't worry about _____ . We have _____ taking care of it now.*

By Relationship-Building and Team-Building
Good morning! How are you?

Thank you! This will help me do my new job better.

I'm calling you instead of sending an e-mail to discuss this issue because this is the first time we are dealing with it.

Can I offer you _____?

Did you know _____ is available? It has helped me greatly.

Check our track record. We have mastered more difficult company restructures before. For example, _____ .

We are the best!

We now have the most experienced team in the industry.

This new structure will help us move beyond the challenges of the old organization.

This is a team effort. We all stay until the job is done.

I'd like to recognize our collective effort by all going out for _____ together.

By Recognizing and Celebrating Progress
Let's go to lunch and celebrate _____ .

I couldn't have done it without your expertise. I'm glad you are on our new team!

I have never seen this done as well as you did it! You are a real asset to our new team. I am particularly impressed by _____ .

This _____ is a terrific sign of progress. We are nearly there! The transition to the new _____ is moving along very well.

I just spoke to _____ , and he/she had nothing but good things to say about you. He/she is really glad you are the new _____ and was particularly impressed by _____ .

By Showing Trust and Support

I'm behind you on that decision!

Don't hesitate to approach me if you have a question or an issue.

You can call me at any time.

I'll take care of that for you.

This is a challenge, but you can do it because _____ .

I know you have never done this before, but I'm confident you'll succeed because _____ .

There is no one I trust more to do this than you because _____ .

I like your input! Let's try it.

I would never have thought of that, but I love your suggestion. Let's try it.

I don't care about how you do it. I just would like to get _____ (result).

By Providing Learning Opportunities

I'm giving you this assignment because I think it will prepare you well for _____ , which will be key to our new structure.

I am counting on you for the long term, which is why I suggest you take _____ training.

Yes, you made a mistake. Only people who do nothing don't make mistakes! New structure implementation requires risk-taking and experimenting. Thanks for trying!

Yes, we didn't succeed with _____, but it was worth trying. Let's see what we learned from it.

Let's focus on what's working and how we can leverage that for the new environment.

By Making Decisions Expeditiously
We want to make a decision on _____ now!

I'm calling _____ and will get back to you with an answer/a decision by tomorrow.

Let's have a meeting this afternoon to decide on _____ so we can move forward.

This issue will be taken care of by tomorrow. I'm not delaying its resolution!

By Including and Involving People
Since this new _____ will impact you, I want to consult with you before I decide. What do you think?

Part of the reason that you are now on our team is that you know more than anyone else about _____. I trust your judgment. Tell me how you think we should proceed.

I don't have the answer. Please discuss this with _____. The two of you will decide together.

By Relieving Stress and Having Fun
We will meet weekly at _____ for "new structure" drinks and food.

Let's cut out early today.

Let's shut off our e-mail and BlackBerries for one hour every day.

Let's take a walk/go for a bike ride/play a round of golf/play a game of tennis/play a match of Ping-Pong and discuss that.

Remember to:

> *take a lunch break.*
>
> *work out.*
>
> *breathe.*
>
> *take note of what's on your mind and discuss your concerns with somebody you trust.*
>
> *take the time to ask yourself, "What are the things I enjoy doing? Am I doing enough of them?"*
>
> *make a joke. It's a great way to relieve stress.*
>
> *take some time every day to hang out with fun-loving people.*

Coaching Around Emotions

Someone Having Outbursts

The implementation of a new structure and its accompanying changes trigger a lot of stress and emotions. Expressing emotions is a productive way of assimilating to change.

Judging by the incident(s) that have occurred over the past few days/weeks, it appears as though you are under a lot of stress. I was wondering:

> *Can you tell me what's going on?*
>
> *Was there something they/we said that triggered your outburst?*
>
> *What do you fear will happen based on the changes we are implementing?*
>
> *What is it about the change that is stressing you out?*

Going forward, we need to ensure that you can manage your emotions in a constructive way. What can we do to:

> *help prevent this from happening in the future?*
>
> *make you feel better about your role in the changes?*
>
> *reduce your stress level?*
>
> *focus your attention on the positive aspects of the changes?*

Someone Working Too Hard

I have observed that you have been working a lot of long hours. I know that you are still performing several functions of your old job at the same time that you have taken on the responsibilities of your new job, and I understand that you may be overstretched in this time of change. Let's discuss this:

> *How do you feel about this?*
>
> *Can you keep your current pace up for another six or more months?*
>
> *What, if anything, could you off-load to someone else on the team?*
>
> *Are there any functions you are performing that are not adding value to the company that you could drop?*
>
> *Are there any deadlines you could delay?*
>
> *Would it help if I provided you with any new tools/additional software/a BlackBerry?*

I appreciate how engaged you are and your commitment to our success. On the other hand, please know that I'm here to support you if you are feeling overloaded.

**Someone Who Says He/She Is on Board with
the Project But Doesn't Take Initiative**
*I hear you saying that you support the new structure. However,
I have noticed that you have not made any progress on any of
the assignments related to the new structure. What's going on?*

*By not taking action, you run the risk of losing credibility with
me/your direct reports/our customers.*

*I understand that we are in a period of transition, but we need
employees who are engaging in the right conversations and
taking the right action to ensure the implementation of the new
structure.*

Do you understand what I mean?

Do you feel like I am treating you fairly?

**Someone Who Says We Don't Have
Enough Resources to Succeed**
*I hear you. This restructuring is challenging, and we have
limited resources.*

*You know, I hadn't considered that. Let's take a few minutes and
examine your concerns in detail.*

*Given that we can't get expand our budget, are not authorized
to hire more employees, and have to live with the technology as
it stands, how can we succeed within our constraints?*

*Our job as leaders/managers/employees is to make the new
structure work within our constraints.*

What else can I do to support your success?

Someone Avoiding Work/Not Engaged
I have noticed lately that you are not as involved as I would like you to be/you used to be. You are not:

> *showing up to meetings.*
> *participating in meetings.*
> *contributing with your ideas.*
> *meeting deadlines.*

What is going on?

We need you on board for this restructuring to work. How can I help get you fully engaged again?

Someone Who Is Impatient
The implementation of a new structure and its accompanying changes trigger a lot of work, stress, and emotions. Each individual reacts to company restructurings differently. I have observed that you are adapting to the change exceptionally well. You have already begun operating within the parameters of the new structure. Thank you!

At the same time, I have noticed that you have grown impatient with those who have not yet assimilated to the changes. I was wondering:

> *if you are aware that you have been behaving in this manner.*
> *how the slow reaction of others impacts you.*
> *why you are getting antsy with your colleagues.*

Understand that other people need more time to get used to the parameters of the new structure. I invite you to try to be a little bit more patient with those who are still adjusting to the change. Are you willing to try that?

Someone Who Is Overwhelmed

I hear you and understand your feelings. I too have been faced with challenging situations that have caused me to feel overwhelmed.

You are right; there is a lot to do and work can seem overwhelming at times.

Please tell me what you have on your plate.

Are there other things, perhaps outside of work, that are getting in your way?

Let's assign priorities. We can also agree to very short-term milestones and then advance one step at a time.

What else can I do to support you? Is there anybody else who could help you?

I'm very happy with your contributions, and I'll support you in any way I can.

Someone Who Asks Too Many Questions and Seems Inflexible

I noticed that you are spending a lot of time trying to find answers to questions that we may not have answers to. For example, _____ .

We are losing time because you are waiting on answers to questions that are unanswerable at this stage. For example, _____ .

I know that we don't have all the information/all the answers to every single question that has arisen. How much is this bothering you?

We need to make the best decisions we can as we move forward. However, sometimes we have to move forward before we know all the potential ramifications that may arise from our actions/decisions. To wait would be too risky/too costly/no option.

I suggest that you try to find your own answer to every question you have. Don't hesitate to run your solutions by me if you need to.

There is no perfect prescription for the challenges we are facing. We will be living in ambiguity for a while and need to do our best with what we know.

Someone Who Keeps Doing Tasks of His/Her Former Role
I have noticed that you are continuing to do your old job as if nothing has changed. Let discuss this briefly:

> *Can you help me better understand what is going on?*
>
> *Let's review your new job description and see what questions you have.*
>
> *Let's develop a step-by-step transition plan.*

Letting go is hard. We all struggle to leave behind things we know for things that we are unfamiliar with. I understand that you feel a sense of obligation to the team and projects you have been a part of for so long.

The faster you can transition into your new role, the faster the new organization will be given the chance to succeed.

Someone Who Believes the Change Is Incompatible with Company Culture
I understand that each change we make as a company is unique and requires a customized approach. Let's discuss this some more:

> *Are you saying that you think this is a good idea for others but is incompatible with the way you do business here? What have you tried that hasn't worked?*
>
> *We need to focus on what we can do and what will work. What do we need to do to make it work here?*

We need to be creative. Since you know that your preferred approach is not an option, what would be your second choice?

What do you fear will happen as a result of our new structure?

How can we mitigate some of the negative consequences you fear might arise as a result of this new structure?

Let's look at each of your fears and determine their legitimacy. Then let's look at how we can creatively reduce the chances that these proposed problems will occur.

Someone Overly Concerned with Status and Less Concerned with Change

I have observed that you:

have not yet changed your e-mail signature to reflect your new title.

are not using your new business cards.

have not yet changed your voice mail message to reflect your new title.

are still introducing yourself to customers with your old title.

have not yet accepted your new title.

have not yet tried out your new title and instead insist that it is inconsistent with your job responsibilities.

Your reaction suggests to me that you support the change and what we are trying to achieve but do not agree with your change of title. Is this correct?

It seems to me that you are primarily concerned with a potential loss of status. What's really going on?

Were you hoping that the changes would unfold exactly as they have, with the exception of your new title?

There is a considerable upside to your new position, and it will be a terrific opportunity for you because _____ . What else can I do to help you overcome your sense of loss of status?

Someone Who Says the Change Is Not Going Far Enough

You are right. More could be done. However, the perfect is the enemy of the good. We have to be pragmatic and start somewhere.

As we move forward with our implementation of the new structure, I'm collecting suggestions of what else could be done to improve what we have. What are your ideas?

What I have captured is _____ . Does this accurately summarize your ideas?

In the meantime, are the changes that we are currently implementing clear to you?

I urge you to be patient and follow our step-by-step approach to the new structure. Rome wasn't built in a day.

Someone Arguing with Others

It has been brought to my attention that you are frequently getting into arguments with _____ . You did not do this prior to our implementing the new structure, and I certainly do not approve of arguing as a communication tactic. What's going on?

Your repeated arguments put you, the person/people you are arguing with, and the company/department/project/larger team in a difficult spot. Your arguments are:

> *slowing our productivity.*
> *impeding our progress.*
> *having a negative impact on overall morale.*
> *creating tension.*

undermining your authority.

dramatically reducing our efficiency.

preventing us from building an effective team.

This has to stop! How can we achieve this goal?

I need you to look at how you are contributing to this problem.

Would you be interested at looking at some internal or external resources that might help resolve this issue?

Coaching for Skills

New Skills

As a result of the new organizational structure, the scope of your job will expand. Accordingly, there are new skills you should acquire/refresh.

You will be working within an area with which our company has no prior experience. Do you have any thoughts about what new skills you might need to succeed?

I suggest you prioritize your top three developmental needs.

Identify what skills you will need in order to reach your new objectives, as well as the corresponding level of competence you will need to acquire in each.

Because your job now will include _____ , I suggest you:

take an _____ (language) course.

talk to _____ , who will introduce you to _____ technology.

meet with _____ to learn about _____ .

network with thought leaders in our new area.

get _____ certified.

refresh your _____ skills.

read a book about _____.

go to _____ conference/lecture/seminar.

find a mentor for _____.

approach internal and external customers for feedback on
how _____.

brainstorm best practices with your colleagues.

identify technical differences between _____
and _____.

read articles, magazines, and journals that feature case studies
of projects related to your new field of responsibility.

take courses in other areas of business knowledge (finance,
legal, scientific, etc.) or operations to broaden your view.

try to better understand the numbers that _____
(our company/department/division) is tracking.

be certain you understand the new internal policies and
procedures about _____ as well as why these
policies and procedures exist.

Great, so we agreed that you will _____.

New Leadership Skills
**As a result of the new organizational structure, you will be
expected to take on a leadership role. To best prepare for these
new expectations, please:**

acquaint yourself with the organizational chart and our
company's job descriptions.

communicate your job description and goals with your peers/
employees/partners.

spend time with your direct reports. Listen to what they have to
say and share your observations with them.

*clearly document agreements. Intervene as soon as you see
agreements not being respected.*

acknowledge achievements and celebrate success!

*stay up-to-date on company values, policies, and business
strategies. Look for opportunities to support these company
priorities through action.*

*consistently display leadership behavior. The most effective way
to change the behavior of others is to model the behavior
you would like them to exhibit. Therefore, if your peers
and direct reports are not displaying leadership behaviors,
make sure that you are!*

*own up to your errors and mistakes. Most people fear that
if they admit to their shortcomings, others will think less
of them. The reality is that you will be admired for your
honesty and willingness to learn.*

Skill Gaps

*I noticed that you are struggling to maintain the higher level of
quality/output/accuracy/speed that our new structure requires.
For example, I noticed that _____, whereas the
expectation is that you _____ .*

What:

do you think you are lacking?

do you think we can do to help you?

would best support you?

training do you think would help?

is interfering?

Who:

in your team/department/company could coach you on that?

*has excelled in this area before that you could turn to as an
example?*

is a thought leader/consultant in this area that you can turn to as an example?

Great, so we agreed that you _____.

Coaching for Flexibility and Adaptability

Offering Direction and Support

Implementing the new structure is a big job. We are all contributing to the success of the new structure. Specifically we will need you to:

> *adapt to your revised job requirements.*
> *be willing to take on new tasks and reprioritize others.*
> *have an open mind and remain as flexible as possible.*
> *quickly build productive relationships with new employees.*
> *help others implement the new structure.*

I know this can seem like a lot.

How are you coping with the stress of our new organizational structure/leader/teammates/roles/responsibilities/processes?

How are you finding time to balance business and the rest of your life?

Are there people on your new team you can turn to for advice and support?

How do you normally adapt to change?

Is there anything I can do to help you be more adaptable?

Here are some pieces of advice and tips on how to build your "change muscles" within this new structure:

> *Apply proactive thinking by considering how your decisions will impact our new structure and revised team configurations.*

*Identify people whom you trust that you can go to if you're not
sure or are worried.*

*Speak up if you are unclear about your level of responsibility or
accountability.*

*Be open to the opinions and approaches of your new
teammates. During this restructuring, the combined
ideas of you and your colleagues will help fine-tune this
organization and its processes.*

*Be willing to adjust your approach to your work as business
processes change.*

*Maintain your existing relationships with colleagues across
hierarchies, geographies, and functions at the same time
that you work to build new partnerships.*

Addressing Performance Problems

Before any discussion of performance problems, you need to set up a
meeting with the employee in question and tell him or her what the
meeting will be about. Bringing someone into your office without fair
warning and time to prepare for the conversation is unfair and will
reduce the productivity of the conversation.

Someone Not Following New Guidelines/New Job Profiles
*I'd like to schedule a meeting with you on _____ to
revisit _____ .*

*During our last meeting we talked about how you have not
been living up to your new role/the new company guidelines.*

You agreed to:

include _____ in your decision-making process.

check with me before committing to _____ .

distribute your updated job profile to all relevant team members.

send a status report on _____ to _____ by _____ .

go to _____ and inform him/her that you are no longer responsible for _____ , which will now be handled by _____ .

We also documented our discussion in this meeting note/e-mail.

Unfortunately you have not upheld our prior agreement. For instance, I observed/heard that you _____ when _____ with _____ .

At our last meeting, we discussed the negative impact your failure to follow the new company guidelines/live up to your new job profile has had on the company's ability to effectively implement the restructuring project. Among other concerns, it:

slows down the restructuring process.

commits us to responsibilities that are no longer within our domain.

confuses our information-gathering efforts.

has a negative impact on our team dynamics.

casts a negative light on our team/department/region.

Would you mind telling me your view of what is going wrong?

If I hear you right, you are saying that _____ .

I see this differently because _____ .

Our agreement needs to be honored in the future. Let's discuss how we can ensure that you can uphold it and get back on track.

Do you agree?

Are you willing to recommit to this agreement?

Are you willing and able to execute all the actions we have discussed and captured?

Is there any additional support I can provide?

Is there anything else we should know about that could prevent you from fulfilling these expectations?

Let's schedule a meeting on _____ to check on your progress.

Someone Not Taking Ownership
During our last meeting we talked about how you have not been taking ownership of _____.

You agreed to:

> *"walk the talk" and uphold commitments that you made during our meeting on _____.*
> *approach your team to _____.*
> *schedule a meeting with _____ to _____.*
> *brainstorm three ways to further promote implementing the new structure in your region/department/team.*
> *proactively respond to employee requests and develop a new _____ that is aligned with our new structure.*
> *draft new job profiles for your direct reports.*
> *meet with your direct reports and assign them short-term goals that align with the new structure.*

We also documented our discussion in this meeting note/e-mail.

Unfortunately you have not upheld our prior agreement. For instance, I have been informed by our Human Resources representative that more than one of your direct reports has called to ask for further detail on their new job titles and descriptions.

At our last meeting, we discussed the negative impact your failure to take ownership has had on the company's ability to effectively implement the restructuring project. Among other concerns, it:

> *slows down the restructuring process.*
>
> *negatively impacts employee morale.*
>
> *unnecessarily creates ambiguity and anxiety.*
>
> *casts a negative light on our team/department/region.*
>
> *casts a negative light on the entire restructuring initiative.*

Would you mind telling me your view of what is going wrong?

If I hear you right, you are saying that _____.

I see this differently because _____.

Our agreement needs to be honored in the future. Let's discuss how we can ensure that you can uphold it and get back on track.

Do you agree?

Are you willing to recommit to this agreement?

Are you willing and able to execute all the actions we have discussed and captured?

Is there any additional support I can provide?

Is there anything else we should know about that could prevent you from fulfilling these expectations?

Let's schedule a meeting on _____ to check on your progress.

Rallying Teams

Goals

I am proud of our new team and its members and appreciate your individual and collective experience and track records. In order to succeed we all need to be pulling in the same direction. After all, we play an important role in ensuring the success of this new structure. There is a lot we can gain from the success of the new structure, such as:

profit and rewards.

visibility.

career opportunities.

exposure to cutting-edge experiences/technologies/practices.

learning about _____.

travel.

expanded networking opportunities with our new colleagues.

Team Objectives

Our team/departmental/divisional/regional/functional goals are to:

consistently satisfy our customers.

generate revenue of $_____.

reduce cost of goods sold to $_____.

increase website traffic by _____ percent.

develop _____ number of new products by _____.

increase market share to _____ percent.

increase compliance in our usage of _____ to _____ by _____.

grow by _____ percent by _____.

We each have our own role to play in this restructuring. Our individual goals each support the larger team/department/ division/region/function goals.

Can you tell me what you understand the team goals to be?

Can you tell me what you understand your role and responsibilities to be?

Teamwork Principles
While every individual plays a unique role in this restructuring, we can't forget that we also are all members of this team. We need to work together to add value to each other and to the larger team's results. Specifically:

> *Each one of us depends on other team members to do their parts! Follow through on your commitments to each other. Be accountable to each other. We sink or swim together!*
>
> *Look out for each other and identify when another team member needs support.*
>
> *Tell each other what you need.*
>
> *Help others recognize how your area of responsibility compliments and supports theirs.*

I will evaluate your success based on how well you support your individual team members as well as the overall team.

Take ownership. Encourage your team members to put forth their top performances and break down barriers by:

> *asking for feedback.*
>
> *giving feedback.*
>
> *sharing what has been working for you.*
>
> *sharing information.*
>
> *sharing ideas.*

sharing observations.

sharing learning.

connecting your team members to your networks.

Listen to each other by:

being certain you fully understand the needs and concerns of others before stating your case.

being respectful of opinions and approaches that differ from your own.

Give credit to each other's contributions.

Address conflicts directly and as they occur. Escalate them if they are irresolvable.

Team Code of Conduct
Given this new challenge, how can we continue to best:

share information?

make good decisions quickly?

assign tasks?

leverage each other's strength?

support each other in pursuing our interests?

exchange feedback in a timely and effective manner?

share what has been working for you?

share information?

share ideas?

share observations?

share learning?

connect to each other's network?

resolve conflicts?

Team Optimization

What is the one thing you most need from the team in order to succeed in this new environment?

Let's take some time to discuss each other's responsibilities and how they overlap.

Go speak to _____ who can explain to you how he/she does _____.

Ask your team members to be specific about what they need from you to succeed.

I'd like each of us to put together a one-page summary of our skills, knowledge, and experiences and share it with the team.

Take the time to identify your peers' skills, knowledge, experiences, contacts, attitudes, and so on.

When making requests of one other, always be clear: What do I need? Why do I need it? By when do I need it? Why do I need you?

Pick up the phone! Talk live as often as possible.

Chapter 3

Perfect Phrases for Communicating a New Project

Special project assignments are so common these days that leaders often forget being assigned to one is a change—a change in priorities, time allocation, and even work relationships. Additionally, the challenges of projects are further amplified in today's workplace through the virtual configuration of project teams. This can include multiple offices, time zones, and even languages. In this chapter we highlight key issues resulting from project assignments and how to handle them to maximize productivity. We recommend also consulting "Communicating Change Virtually" in Chapter 1 to obtain valuable hints for making smart decisions about media use when leading projects (i.e., e-mail, web meetings, phone calls, and face-to-face meetings).

Announcing Change

Project Overview
The project is called _____ .

The goals of the project are _____ .

The key deliverables and deadlines include _____ .

_____ *is the sponsor of this project.*

The project team includes _____ .

Their roles and responsibilities are _____ .

The budget is $ _____ *and comes from*
_____ .

The reason this project is important is _____ .

Individual Buy-In
We want you on this project because:

> *of your experience with this customer/department/technology/*
> *region.*
>
> *of your success in the past with related projects.*
>
> *you have extra capacity right now.*
>
> *we see this as a developmental opportunity where you will gain*
> *important experience regarding* _____ .
>
> *this will allow you to expand your network in the organization.*

If this project assignment isn't appealing to the employee, you may need to add:

> *I know that this is not what you wanted to be assigned to. I*
> *know you wanted to be assigned to* _____ *project*
> *because* _____ . *However, we put you on this project*
> *because* _____ . *How can we create a situation where*
> *this is a win for you also?*

Responding to Questions

How Are We Going to Juggle This Project with Everything Else Going On?

I am perfectly aware that this project is putting an additional strain on us. We expect that this is within the range of additional work you can take on.

In terms of priorities, this project is:

> *now the first priority for the next _____ (period of time).*
>
> *something to do in between; however, it must be done by _____ .*
>
> *something to do if you have time.*
>
> *a high priority, but _____ shouldn't suffer.*

Overcoming Fear

Someone Who Is Overwhelmed

I hear that this is challenging for you and indeed some of these demands may look overwhelming. Would you mind updating me on your other projects?

OK. Let's talk about priorities and focus. As we discussed, your priorities for the next _____ (period of time) are _____ .

It might be helpful if you focused first on _____ . Then, check back with me to discuss how it went.

I know that there is a lot to do. I am confident we can work through this because:

> *the deadlines seem doable.*
>
> *you have an excellent team working with you.*
>
> *you succeeded at _____ , and this is a similar situation.*

you have the right attitude to pull this off.

a lot of work has been done already.

Given the importance of this project, if you can pull this off, I will acknowledge your extra effort by:

informing _____ of your success.

lobbying to get you on _____ project.

treating you to dinner.

getting the budget to let you go to that conference later this year.

Please don't hesitate to check back with me if you need anything.

Someone Who Is Scared He/She Doesn't Have the Necessary Skills

I understand your concern about having the skill set needed right now. You are not alone. Most of us will be learning as we go along.

Tell me what part of the project you are struggling with and what you think you need to succeed.

We will make sure that you get the appropriate coaching/mentoring/training to succeed.

Creating Urgency

Keeping the Momentum

It is critical that we succeed in this new project so that we can:

stay number one in the market.

become number one in the market by _____ .

grow our business by _____ .

diversify by adding _____ .

expand into _____ .

reduce our response time to _____ .

improve our operational efficiencies.

make _____ happy.

comply with (new) legal requirements.

By doing so, this will help you/our team to:

increase the amount of your/their salary/bonuses.

save your/their job(s).

create more career and development opportunities.

Addressing Power Struggles and Career Issues

How Does This Project Help Your Career?
This project will help you to:

get exposure and broaden your understanding of sales/ marketing/operations/research.

get to know key company decision makers.

potentially make more money in the future and/or be more marketable based on the new skills you're learning.

gain experience leading teams.

gain experience working with other regions/countries.

get inspired and inspire others.

work closely with _____ , who is a leading expert/ major player/recognized personality in the field.

get exposure to the latest technology.

work with new/key customers.

be involved in the biggest growth market.

learn about a new strategic area.

Clarifying Roles and Responsibilities

This project will impact your current roles and responsibilities.

We planned that this project will take _____ percent of your time.

Your current responsibilities are going to change as follows:

> *We are delaying the deadline for _____ .*
>
> *You have _____ helping you with _____ .*
>
> *We hired an outside vendor for _____ .*

Your performance goals/bonus/compensation will be adjusted accordingly.

Or

Accordingly, we have to reassign some of your current workload. Let's take a look at your current work assignments and determine what shifts to make.

Or

Let's go through your current obligations and see how to prioritize them and what we can do to support you.

Communicating Individual Objectives

Clarifying What Is Expected

I'm referring back to the conversations we already have had and reiterating the objectives of our project. They are _____ .

We have talked about your project role and the responsibilities that come with it. I'm counting on you to bring this project to a successful start/completion.

These are your initial/short-term goals. Within the next
_____ *days, I'd like you to:*

> contact the project leader to get oriented.
>
> familiarize yourself with project background documentation.
>
> gather any relevant data.
>
> refresh your knowledge in the subject matter area of the project.
>
> set up the project charter.
>
> assemble the full team for a kickoff.
>
> set goals with each project team member.
>
> come up with a detailed project plan.
>
> design a change management strategy.
>
> analyze the budget and related limitations for our project.

Empowering Employees

Individual Contributors

I have told you a lot about this new project, its objectives, budget, and milestones. We now need you to bring it to life by:

> being certain you understand the project objectives and the rational behind the project.
>
> being aware of other factors (governmental, environmental, economic, etc.) that influence the project.
>
> trying to thoroughly understand the metrics as they relate to project success.
>
> bringing your business knowledge to the project team meetings and sharing what you know will work.
>
> seeking support from me when you sense a conflict between your traditional responsibilities and your project involvement.

Leaders

We have discussed a lot about this new project, its objectives, budget, and milestones. We now need you to bring it to life by:

understanding and, where necessary, clarifying roles and responsibilities as far as decision making and accountability are concerned.

reviewing your resources and seeing how you can reallocate them to accommodate the new project.

being aware of other (outside) obligations of your project team members.

clearly documenting agreements and intervening as soon as you see agreements not being respected.

keeping me and other key stakeholders informed of commitments and project progress.

involving all stakeholders as early as possible.

learning/applying techniques to facilitate effective meetings.

Keeping People Motivated

By Providing Clarity of Vision/Direction

The project charter is to _____ .

Your primary objectives/requirements are to _____ .
_____ is out of scope.

Focus more on _____ rather than _____ .

The next major milestone is _____ .

We are not aiming to create the perfect solution.

We'll be measured on _____ .

This project has priority over/supersedes _____ .

Escalate any issues to _____ as soon as they occur.

As captured in the project charter you are responsible for _____ , and _____ is responsible for _____ .

Don't worry about _____ . We have _____ taking care of it.

By Relationship-Building and Team-Building
Please introduce yourselves and tell each other about your backgrounds.

Let's start by talking about our hopes and fears for the project.

What did you learn from your last project that we could implement here?

Hello, _____ , how is the project progressing? What are you learning? Are you having fun? Are you meeting interesting people?

Can I offer you _____ ?

Did you know _____ is available? It has helped me greatly.

I'd like to recognize our collective effort by all going out for _____ together.

By Recognizing and Celebrating Progress
Let's go to lunch and celebrate _____ .

We couldn't have done it without your expertise, I'm glad you are on our project team!

I have never seen this done as well as you did it! You are a real asset to our project team. I am particularly impressed by _____ .

This _____ is a terrific sign of progress. We are nearly there! This project will be a smashing success!

I just spoke to _____ , and she/he had nothing but good things to say about _____ . She/he was particularly impressed by _____ .

By Showing Trust and Support
I'm behind you on that decision!

Don't hesitate to approach me if you have a question or an issue.

You can call me at any time.

I'll take care of that for you.

I like your input! Let's try it.

I would never have thought of that, but I love your suggestion. Let's try it.

I don't care how you do it. I just would like to get _____ (result).

This is a team effort. We'll all make ourselves available to get this deliverable done.

By Providing Learning Opportunities
I'm putting you on this project because I think it will prepare you well for _____ , which is key to our business.

Let's focus on what's already working and how we can leverage it for the rest of the project.

Please research best practices in this _____ so we can apply them to the project.

Partner up with _____ to learn from him/her.

Take a _____ course to become more efficient with our project methodology.

By Making Decisions Expeditiously

Let's add _____ to the agenda for our next status meeting.

We need to address this conflict. What is taking priority? I will call our project sponsor now.

Let's refer to our governance document to find the answer we are looking for.

I'm calling a _____ meeting. The participants are _____, and here is the agenda. Please prepare for the meeting according to the assignments on the agenda.

By Including and Involving People

We have assembled a cross-regional/cross-disciplinary team to make sure all views are represented today. You are the ambassador of your area, both in representing your view on the project and reporting back to your respective constituencies.

Part of the reason that you are on this project team is that you know more than anyone about _____. I trust your judgment. Tell me how we should proceed.

I don't have the answer. Please discuss this with _____. The two of you will decide together.

By Relieving Stress and Having Fun
*We meet once a _____ at _____ for an
informal project get-together.*

*Let's shut off our e-mail and BlackBerries during all our project
meetings.*

*Let's take a walk/go for a bike ride/play a round of golf/
play a game of tennis/play a match of Ping-Pong after
finishing _____ .*

*Let's start/end each meeting with a joke. It's a great way to
relieve stress. The funniest one of each meeting gets an award.*

As a best practice, remember to build and nurture relationships
with the superiors of project team members. You will need their help
to keep up team member motivation, including addressing conflict-
ing priorities and handling any performance issues.

Coaching Around Emotions

**Someone Who Says He/She Is on Board with
the Project But Doesn't Take Initiative**
*I hear you saying you want to be on the project, but I have not
seen you taking any initiative.*

*Your lack of initiative is resulting in negative consequences.
You are:*

> *losing precious time/delaying the implementation of
> dependent tasks.*
>
> *losing credibility.*
>
> *demotivating the project team.*
>
> *putting my objectives at risk with my manager.*

We need people on the project who are ready to take action now.

Can you share with me what is happening?

So let's recap. Going forward, you are going to _____ and I am going to _____ .

Someone Complaining About Not Having Enough People/Technology/Budget for This Project
I hear you. This project is challenging and we have limited resources.

You know, I hadn't considered that. Let's take a few minutes and examine that in detail:

> *Our job as leaders/managers/employees is to make it work within our constraints.*
>
> *What else can I do to support your success?*
>
> *You know the limitations we are working within. What can we do to help you move forward?*
>
> *We can't get more budget or people, and we have to live with the technology as it stands. What can we do within those constraints?*
>
> *You are right, we could use more people/budget/technology. We don't have it. However, doing nothing is not an option! What would you suggest?*

Someone Who Is Constantly Opposing Project Methodology and Policies
This methodology is indeed one of many that have been successfully used in similar projects. I understand that you may be more familiar with one of the others and are struggling to adjust to the new requirements and processes. At the same time, we need you to be using our approved methodology.

What do we need to do to achieve this?

What, if any, coaching/mentoring/training could help get you up to speed?

We are relying on your ingenuity, experience, and professionalism to bring this project to a successful completion. I am confident you can make it happen.

What do we need to do to get your commitment?

Someone Who Is Overwhelmed
I hear you and understand your feelings. I too have been faced with challenging situations that have caused me to feel overwhelmed.

I am here to help you.

You are right; there is a lot to do and work can seem overwhelming at times.

Let's take a look at your situation and see what we can do. Please tell me what you have on your plate. Now let's assign priorities.

Let's agree to very short-term milestones and goals and then advance one step at a time.

Are there other things, perhaps outside of work, that are preventing you from contributing?

What else can I do to support you?

Is there anybody else we should involve?

We need your duties completed, and I will support you as best I can to get this accomplished.

Coaching for Skills

New Skills for Project Team Members
With this project your job is expanding. Accordingly, there are new skills you should acquire/refresh.

Do you have any thoughts about what new skills you might need to succeed in this project?

Which skills would you need to brush up on?

You might want to consider what skills you need in order to reach your project objectives and the corresponding level of competence. From there, we could come up with a development plan.

Because the project will require you to _____, and based on what we have discussed, I suggest you:

> *talk to the team leader/team members about _____.*
>
> *get an introduction to _____ technology.*
>
> *meet with _____ to learn about _____.*
>
> *get _____ certified.*
>
> *refresh your _____ skills.*
>
> *read a book about _____.*
>
> *find a mentor for _____.*
>
> *identify technical differences between _____ and _____.*
>
> *read articles, magazines, and journals that feature case studies of similar projects.*
>
> *be certain you understand the related internal policies and procedures about _____ and why they exist.*

Great, so what we agreed to is that you _____.

New Skills for Project Managers
With this project you will need to apply very solid project management skills.

> *Do you have the necessary skills and experience? Please tell me about them.*
>
> *I'd suggest you acquire/refresh project management skills.*
>
> *You might want to consider what project management skills you will need. From there, we could come up with a development plan.*

To develop/refresh those project management skills I suggest you:

> *obtain a solid working knowledge of project management principles by reading a book, attending a conference, or undergoing formal training.*
>
> *talk to _____ about how to create concise, easy-to-understand project plans and how to establish clear timetables and budgets.*
>
> *not reinvent the wheel. Use past project templates as a starting point.*
>
> *ask another professional whose experience related to planning you admire to mentor you.*
>
> *create a stakeholder list. Be clear about the expectations of each stakeholder. If you are not clear, ask the stakeholder.*
>
> *plan and discuss alternative scenarios.*
>
> *discuss best practices and evaluate new planning and project management tools, for example, by tapping into your industry association or alumni network.*

Great, so what we agreed to is that you _____ .

Projects often go through crisis or even fail because project managers underestimate the importance of relationships. This includes building good relationships with your team members, and they in turn building them with each other. I suggest you

> block out enough time at the start and throughout the project for relationship building.
>
> regularly ask your team members how things are going.
>
> address conflicts quickly before they become destructive.
>
> put yourself in your project team's shoes and remember to consider what is in it for them.

Skill Gaps

I noticed that you are struggling with the higher level of quality/output/accuracy/speed needed. For example, I noticed that _____. Whereas the expectation is that you _____.

What:

> do you think you are lacking?
>
> do you think we can do to help you?
>
> would best support you?
>
> training do you think would help?
>
> is interfering?

Who:

> is on your team/department/company who could coach you on that?
>
> has excelled in this before us?
>
> is a thought leader/consultant in the area?

Some tips to keep in mind are:

> remember to confirm requests, agreements, and action plans in writing.
>
> track and monitor progress with tangible milestones.

> keep a library of effective approaches, templates, and resources you can call on.
>
> start small! Once you are comfortable with managing small projects, tackle projects with continuously increasing sizes.
>
> be the first to raise concerns or negative consequences. Be sure you also provide potential solutions. Most people avoid raising bad news—yet those who do and who provide positive solutions gain credibility.

Great, so what we agreed to is that you _____.

Coaching for Flexibility and Adaptability

Offering Direction and Support
This new project requires you to:

> expect changing project requirements and a changing project team configuration. You also will need to be flexible to respond to these changes.
>
> adapt to two concurring job requirements (your traditional job and the project).
>
> be willing to take on new tasks and reprioritize others.
>
> have an open mind and show flexibility when applying new approaches, methodologies, and skills.
>
> quickly build productive relationships with new people.

This could be a lot to handle. I just want to check in and see how you feel about it.

> Have you been in similar projects before?
>
> How are you coping with the stress that comes with the project?
>
> How are you finding time to balance business and the rest of your life?
>
> Whom do you turn to for advice and support?

Is there anything I can do to support you adapting to this new project?

Here are some ideas on how you can more easily adapt to changing project environments:

> *Take time to prioritize tasks.*
>
> *Celebrate your and the project team's achievements.*
>
> *Apply proactive thinking by anticipating the project's future needs and potential new developments.*
>
> *Identify people you trust whom you can go to if you're not sure or worried.*
>
> *Speak up if your tasks or milestones are unclear.*
>
> *Look for tasks you can delegate to other people.*
>
> *Look for people you think can flexibly chip in if the need arises.*

Addressing Performance Problems

Someone Who Doesn't Meet Deadlines

I'd like to schedule a meeting with you on _____ to revisit _____ .

Unfortunately we need to have a discussion because you have not been meeting deadlines.

You agreed to:

> *carefully read the project plan.*
>
> *organize your work in a way that allows you to meet deadlines.*
>
> *reprioritize other tasks.*
>
> *update your software to be compatible with _____ , to accelerate how quickly you can _____ , and to increase the ease of exchanging documents _____ .*
>
> *talk to _____ , who is a master in managing tough deadlines.*

I have the notes I took during this meeting in front of me. I assume you have a copy with you also, right?

Regrettably, there has been a slippage again. The last milestone was not met.

I assume I don't need to explain to you again the impact those missed deadlines have on the success of the project and the morale of the project team.

What happened this time?

If I hear you right, you are saying that _____ .

All of us are frustrated by this situation and are becoming increasingly impatient. You have to fix this and account for all extenuating factors in your work plans. The existing project plan must be honored. How do you suggest we avoid any further slippages?

Are you willing to recommit to this agreement?

Are you willing and able to execute all the actions we have discussed and captured above?

Is there any additional support I can provide?

Let's schedule a meeting on _____ to check in and monitor progress.

Someone Who Violates Formal Project Rules
We met last time to discuss your "creative" interpretation of our project guidelines.

I emphasized to you that complying with all the formalities of our approach is not optional but a must because _____ .

You agreed to:

> revisit the project guidelines.
>
> go back to your notes and your documentation of the project kickoff.
>
> fix all the problems we discussed then.
>
> consult with _____ , who has a very solid understanding of our methodology.
>
> use the template provided at kickoff.

We both also have a written documentation of our agreement.

I have been confronted with more rules violations. Let's just briefly recapture—as we did last time—the negative impact this has on our project. It:

> is jeopardizing our company's compliance with governmental/ industry regulations.
>
> is impeding the exchange of our plans and specs with other vendors and suppliers.
>
> makes communication with other team members more difficult.
>
> inhibits our ability to capture your work in our software system and, therefore, makes the software output unreliable.
>
> sets a very bad example for the team.

Would you mind sharing your point of view?

If I hear you right, you are saying that _____ .

I see this differently because _____ .

All our guidelines need to be honored in the future. Let's discuss how we can assure that you indeed can live up to them and that you will get back on track. Do you agree?

Are you willing to recommit to this agreement?

Are you willing and able to execute all the actions we have discussed and captured above?

Is there any additional support I can provide?

Is there anything else we should know about that could prevent you from fulfilling your duties?

Let's schedule a meeting on _____ to check in and monitor your progress.

Rallying Teams

Goals
I am excited to work with this new project team! You each bring your own experience and expertise to the table. We need our combined talent to succeed. There is much we all can gain from this project, such as:

> *rewards and recognition.*
>
> *visibility.*
>
> *career opportunities.*
>
> *exposure to cutting-edge experiences/technologies/practices.*
>
> *knowledge about _____ .*
>
> *expanded networking opportunities with our project collaborators.*

Project Team Objectives
Our project team objectives are _____ .

We need to complete the project on time, at the quality level requested, and within budget.

We each have our own role to play. Our individual goals each support the larger team goals.

Roles and responsibilities have been defined in the project charter.

Project Teamwork Principles
We need to focus on how we add value to each other and to the larger team's results. Specifically:

> *We depend on each other to do our parts. Follow through on your commitments to each other. Be accountable to each other. We sink or swim together!*
>
> *Look out for each other, and identify when another team member needs support.*
>
> *Tell each other what you need.*
>
> *Help others see how your area of responsibility complements and supports theirs. And vice versa.*

Take ownership. Encourage each other to exhibit top performances by:

> *asking for feedback.*
>
> *giving feedback.*
>
> *sharing what has been working for you.*
>
> *sharing information.*
>
> *sharing ideas.*
>
> *sharing observations.*
>
> *sharing learning.*

Listen to each other and:

> *be certain you fully understand the needs and concerns of others before stating your case.*
>
> *be respectful of opinions and approaches different from your own.*

Give credit to each other's contributions.

Address conflicts of priorities as they occur and immediately escalate if not resolvable.

Team Code of Conduct
Given this new challenge, how can we continue to best:

> *share information?*
>
> *make good decisions quickly?*
>
> *assign tasks?*
>
> *leverage each other's strength?*
>
> *exchange feedback in a timely and effective manner?*
>
> *share what has been working?*
>
> *share information?*
>
> *share ideas?*
>
> *share observations?*
>
> *share learning?*
>
> *resolve differences of opinion?*
>
> *resolve priority conflicts?*

Team Optimization
We'll be using _____ project planning methodology.

What questions do you have about our project charter, sponsors, scheduling, status reporting, and so on?

What do you need from the team to succeed with your project tasks?

Let's take some time to discuss each other's responsibilities and how they overlap.

Ask team members specific questions about what they need from you to succeed.

I'd like each of us to put together a one-page summary of personal skills, knowledge, and experiences that are relevant to this project.

When making requests of each other, always be clear: What do I need? Why do I need it? By when do I need it? Why do I need you?

Pick up the phone! Talk live as often as possible.

Chapter 4

Perfect Phrases for Communicating as a New Leader

With the arrival of a new boss, employees must essentially start all over again, which is made easier through good two-way communication. Employee productivity is largely built upon the relationship with direct managers: understanding their priorities and point of view, knowing how to read between the lines, and even being able to tell when it's a good time to talk them. Remember also that, as a new leader, your words and actions are watched under a microscope by your team. This chapter provides concrete suggestions for leaders to quicken the pace of relationship-building, business focus, and, therefore, productivity. We also recommend that in addition to following the advice in this chapter, you consult the "Three Most Common Mistakes Leaders Make When Communicating Change" and "Best Practices" sections in Chapter 1.

Announcing Change

Personal Introduction of New Boss or Superior

I am delighted to announce that _____ will be succeeding _____ as the leader of _____ . He/she will start in this capacity effective _____ .

_____ is a very accomplished leader and professional. His/her experience includes _____ (summarize major accomplishments and link to key role requirements).

Personal Introduction by New Boss or Superior to Secure Individual Buy-In

I'd like to tell you a little about my background. (Discuss what you learned at previous positions and how that knowledge relates to the challenges at this company/division/team, as well as personal information about your family, interests, college attended, etc.)

My main principles and values that I think are relevant here are:

> *I need to hear and share bad news on time.*
>
> *Creativity is valued.*
>
> *With a little hard work, we can get a lot done.*
>
> *Mistakes happen, but let's learn from them and improve.*
>
> *Planning pays.*
>
> *I trust and build on my leadership team.*
>
> *I expect us all to do what is right and legal.*
>
> *I delegate duties and responsibilities to empower you to be involved and make decisions.*
>
> *My door is always open, but let's look at solutions and not just problems.*
>
> *Communication is a two-way street.*

You are the closest to the customer, so I am in need of your point of view.

I abide by the 80/20 rule, in that I believe that the perfect is the enemy of the good.

Our priorities for the next three months are:

sales.

margins.

operational efficiencies.

projects.

people.

innovation.

As a best practice, we recommend conducting a stakeholder analysis, which will help identify key priorities and keep employees focused on them. First, list your team's internal and external customers. Next, clarify with your team who these stakeholders are and what they expect. Then confirm with your stakeholders that these expectations are accurate. Finally, regularly track customer satisfaction. This can be done as simply as asking how things are going, sending surveys, or using third-party interviews and focus groups. The data and trends you receive will be a powerful leadership tool, ensuring your team stays focused on key success factors and gets regular feedback on how it is doing. Ultimately, it will remove guesswork and eliminate wishful thinking.

Responding to Questions

Why Didn't We Look Internally?
This position requires someone who has success with _____ .

We started the search internally and were unable to find a candidate who _____ .

We consciously looked externally because we thought someone with a new perspective would be valuable for this position.

Why Was I Not Selected for This Position?
I know you were hoping to get this job. We looked closely at you for this position. You have some great skills and experience. We appreciate your contributions to the company. However, we don't think you are ready yet. We think you need to do _____ to prepare for this kind of position. There will be other opportunities for you.

Or

I know you were hoping to get this job. We looked closely at that. We felt you were not as qualified because:

you did not meet some critical deadlines in the past, such as when _____ .

your performance in the last performance review cycle dropped.

you still need to work on your technical skills, such as _____ .

you are not willing to relocate, which may happen with this position.

you are only able to travel 25 percent, and the position requires more travel than that.

Does My Job Change Now?
It is too early to say. We need to wait until _____ . For sure, I/he/she will be examining how things work. There will be changes.

You may need to add:

You are a key contributor here. We reviewed the team with _____ , and I/he/she is well aware of your past contributions to the team's success.

Also be prepared to answer questions about what the criteria were for selection.

Overcoming Fear

Someone Scared of Losing Power/Influence
It is natural for there to be a "getting to know you" phase. This will take some time. What I have done already is review your personnel file. I am very impressed with your _____ (background, achievements, contributions). I also plan to:

> *pay attention to your contributions and participation in our meetings.*
>
> *listen to your point of view on our business situation.*
>
> *observe your results.*
>
> *join you in customer/project meetings.*
>
> *get feedback from your customers/partners.*
>
> *have weekly one-on-one meetings with you.*

As a reminder, the big picture is _____ . I am looking for someone in your position who:

> *is willing to follow the new vision.*
>
> *speaks up and shares his/her point of view.*

takes initiative.

exercises good judgment.

is a relationship-builder.

gets stuff done.

is trustworthy.

In this new role, you will have:

decision-making power over _____ .

the opportunity to influence _____ .

_____ *and I will continue to involve you*

in _____ .

Creating Urgency

Keeping the Momentum
It is critical that we very quickly establish a productive relationship because:

we are under a lot of pressure from above/our boss/the board/ our customers/the public.

I can't do it alone.

I'd hate to jeopardize all the good work that has been done in the past.

By doing so, you will be in a better position to:

keep your job.

expand your job to include _____ .

create more career and development opportunities such as _____ .

make more money.

get better work/life balance.

have the opportunity to work with _____ *.*

be exposed to _____ *.*

Addressing Power Struggles and Career Issues

What Are Your Career Interests?

Let's start with discussing your career objectives:

> *How did you get to where you are now?*
>
> *Where would you like to be five years from now?*
>
> *What are some of the key factors driving your career aspirations?*
>
> *What, if any, specific roles in the company have you considered?*
>
> *What do you consider your key strengths?*
>
> *Where do you have developmental needs?*
>
> *What is your geographical mobility?*

There may be opportunities to move up, but there are also interesting lateral moves to enable you to gain experience in other functions/industries/divisions.

I am committed to your success and to helping you navigate through the organization.

Clarifying Roles and Responsibilities

I have captured what I understand to be the key elements of your role. It includes:

> *your title.*
>
> *who you're reporting to.*
>
> *your key performance measures.*
>
> *who is on your team.*
>
> *your main responsibilities.*

Let's discuss if and how this differs from what you have been doing until now.

What questions do you have?

Communicating Individual Objectives

Setting Expectations
I'm delighted to have you on my team and am very much looking forward to our collaboration! There is a lot to implement and do, and I'm very keen to get a quick and successful start. Here are my short-term expectations for you. Within the next _____ week(s), I'd like to:

> *bring _____ to a close.*
>
> *get ready to start the new initiative we discussed.*
>
> *put together a brief presentation of your main initiatives, key opportunities, potential challenges, and budget allocations for the rest of the year.*
>
> *have you introduce me to your team.*
>
> *update your performance objectives for the year.*

Empowering Employees

Individual Contributors
I can only achieve my goals with your support. With that in mind:

> *Please take a moment to look over your job description. Make sure you clearly understand your role and your responsibilities. If not, please get back to me by _____ .*
>
> *Focus on what you can achieve and influence. Don't be limited by old ways of doing business.*

Learn how to handle those requests I make of you that are beyond your resources or capabilities by giving me alternative options and saying no in a professional manner.

If you have a question or don't agree with a business decision, speak up! You may be right, but so may I.

Learn about the key indicators (financial, operational, sales, etc.) we are using to track our performance. Ask somebody in accounting, a peer, or your manager to help you analyze these indicators.

Keep me and other key stakeholders informed of your commitments and any progress you make with regard to implementing the new charter.

Please help me appropriately delegate work to you. I would like to delegate as much as possible—but not too much. Let me know how this is going.

Leaders

I can only achieve my goals with your support. With that in mind:

Be crystal clear about what we want to achieve. Share your goals with your peers/direct reports. This will help them take ownership and stay focused.

Look at your new charter and further scope out your tactics.

Spend time with your people. Listen to what they have to say and incorporate their ideas as much as possible.

Find ways to involve people who may not yet have a full understanding of my vision.

Help your team plan learning and development activities to help us achieve our new goals.

Think about how our high-level, overall objectives apply to your business/division/region/department/team. Make sure you define individual objectives accordingly.

Review your resources and reallocate them based on the new charter.

Involve your people, and, within reason, delegate as much as possible.

Regularly review your own and your department's progress on your implementation of the charter.

Keeping People Motivated

By Providing Clarity of Vision/Direction

My new vision for our _____ is _____ .

Our number one priority is _____ .

Your number one objective is _____ .

Our key performance measures are _____ .

Don't worry about _____ . I have _____ taking care of it now.

By Relationship-Building and Team-Building

Good morning! How are you?

Thank you! This will help me do my new job better.

I'm calling you instead of sending an e-mail to discuss this issue since this is the first time we are dealing with this issue.

Can I offer you _____ ?

Check your track record. You all have mastered more difficult situations before. For example, you _____ .

We are the best!

We now have the most experienced team in the industry.

This new approach will help us move beyond the previous challenges you told me about.

This is a team effort. I'll stay here with you until the job is done.

I'd like to recognize our collective effort by all going out for _____ together.

By Recognizing and Celebrating Progress

Let's go to lunch and celebrate _____ .

I couldn't have done it without your expertise. I'm glad you are on my team!

I have never seen this done as well as you did it! You are a real asset to our team. I am particularly impressed by _____ .

This _____ is a terrific sign of progress. The transition to the new _____ is moving along wonderfully.

I just spoke to _____ , and she/he had nothing but good things to say about you. She/he was particularly impressed by _____ .

By Showing Trust and Support

I'm giving you this assignment because it is key to executing my new vision, and I trust you.

I'm behind you on that decision!

Don't hesitate to approach me if you have a question or an issue.

You can call me at any time.

I'll take care of that for you.

This is a challenge, but you can do it because _____ .

I know you have never done that before, but I'm confident you'll succeed because _____ .

There is no one I trust more to do this than you because _____ .

I like your input! Let's try it.

I would never have thought of that, but I love your suggestion. Let's try it.

I don't care about how you do it. I just would like to get _____ (result).

By Providing Learning Opportunities
I am counting on you for the long term. This is why I suggest you take _____ training.

Yes, you made a mistake. It's something I'd expect any engaged person to do. Only people who do nothing don't make mistakes!

Yes, we didn't succeed with _____ . But it was worth trying. Let's see what we learned from it.

Let's focus on what's already working and how we can leverage that for our new priorities.

By Making Decisions Expeditiously
We want to take a decision on that now!

I'm calling _____ and will get back to you with an answer/a decision by tomorrow.

Let's have a meeting this afternoon to decide on _____ so we can move forward.

This issue will be taken care of by tomorrow. I'm not delaying its resolution!

By Including and Involving People

Since this new _____ will impact you, I wanted to consult with you before I make a decision. What do you think?

You are our expert on _____. I trust your judgment. Tell me how we should proceed.

I don't have the answer. Please discuss this with _____. The two of you will decide together.

By Relieving Stress and Having Fun

We will be meeting every _____ at _____ for a team get-together with drinks and food. Please come. The more people who participate, the more fun the gathering will be.

Let's shut off our e-mail and BlackBerries for one day during the weekend.

Let's take a walk/go for a bike ride/play a round of golf/play a game of tennis/play a match of Ping-Pong and discuss that.

Remember to:

> *take a lunch break.*
>
> *work out.*
>
> *breathe.*
>
> *take notes of things on your mind and discuss them with somebody you trust.*
>
> *take the time to ask yourself, "What are the things I enjoy doing? Am I doing enough of them?"*
>
> *make a joke. It's a great way to relieve stress.*
>
> *take some time every day to hang out with fun-loving people.*

Here comes an incentive: For the person who is best at _____ , I will:

wash your car.

serve you lunch.

treat you to lunch.

let you off two hours earlier on Friday.

do cartwheels.

train for a triathlon with you.

switch offices for a day.

give you my parking spot for a week.

allow you to use my car and driver for a day.

let you use the corporate apartment in _____ .

offer a free round of golf for a foursome with our corporate golf membership.

Coaching Around Emotions

Someone Who Says He/She Is on Board but Doesn't Take Initiative

I appreciate you saying you support me. However, what I have observed is that you are often challenging things we are implementing and you seem to prefer doing things the old way. I have the impression that having a new leader is not easy for you. I want to make this work. I need you on my team. How can we improve our collaboration?

I am expecting you to:

clearly communicate our decisions with your team.

walk the talk by _____ .

live up to our values and principles.

leverage your influence as an ambassador for our new initiatives.

Can I get your commitment?

Someone Who Believes the Change Is Incompatible with Company Culture

I understand that you have been with the company/the industry much longer than I have and that you have a lot of experience in the field.

I'm trying to change the way things are being done here. And by doing so, I'm introducing innovation and trying new approaches.

Why aren't you supporting our decisions in the field? For example, _____.

What do we need to do to make this work?

To summarize, you will start _____ and stop _____, and I will _____.

Coaching for Skills

New Skills

With the changes I'm implementing, your job is expanding. Accordingly, there are new skills you should acquire/refresh.

These changes necessitate that you approach your work from a different perspective than what you are used to. What impact does this have on the skills required to excel in your job?

With your new objectives in mind, what skills do you need primarily? And what is the corresponding level of competence you need to succeed?

Because your job now will include _____, I suggest you:

> *take a _____ (language) course.*
> *talk to _____ and get an introduction to _____ technology.*

meet with _____ to learn about _____ .

network with thought leaders in our new area.

get _____ certified.

refresh your _____ skills.

read a book about _____ .

go to _____ conference/lecture/seminar.

find a mentor for _____ .

approach internal and external customers for feedback on how _____ .

brainstorm best practices with your colleagues.

identify technical differences between _____ and _____ .

read articles, magazines, and journals that feature case studies of projects related to your new field of responsibility.

take courses in other areas of business knowledge or operations (i.e., finance, law, science, etc.) to broaden your view.

try to better understand the numbers _____ (our company/department/division) is tracking.

be certain you understand the new internal policies and procedures about _____ and why they exist.

Great, so what we agreed to is that you _____ .

Skill Gaps

I noticed that you are struggling with the higher level of quality/output/accuracy/speed needed. For example, I noticed that _____ , whereas the expectation is that you _____ .

What:

do you think you are lacking?

do you think we can do to help you?

would best support you?

training do you think would help?

is interfering?

I want to encourage you not to just rely on me for feedback but have a "learning" attitude. Here are some things to do:

At the end of each task, ask internal and external customers for feedback on how you met their needs—especially in those areas where you think you can improve.

Be sure you act in a nondefensive way when you receive feedback about improvement areas.

Identify problems as they occur. Address them proactively by discussing them first with me and then with your peers.

Don't avoid or procrastinate issues resolution.

Meet face-to-face, or at least on the phone, as often as reasonable.

Great, so what we agreed to is that you _____.

Coaching for Flexibility and Adaptability

To ensure that my transition into this new leadership role will be as successful as possible, I need you to:

be willing to take on new tasks and reprioritize others.

have an open mind and show flexibility in your approaches.

look for opportunities to initiate changes that are in line with my new vision.

help/support me in promoting my new ideas and approaches.

I know this can be a difficult and emotional time. Let me ask you:

*What are some ways you have succeeded in being flexible in
the past?*

How are you coping with the stress that comes with it?

*How are you finding time to balance business with the rest of
your life?*

Whom do you turn to for advice and support?

How do you normally adapt to change?

Is there anything I can do to support you?

**Here are some pieces of advice and tips on how to better
navigate this transition:**

Be willing to stretch yourself and take on new challenges.

*Learn to say no to me and others. You have to be able to off-
load tasks of lesser urgency or priority.*

*Apply proactive thinking. Anticipate any needs that may arise
as a result of our new charter.*

Speak up if my communication or direction is unclear.

*Speak up if your level of responsibility and accountability is
unclear.*

Addressing Performance Problems

Someone Plowing Forward Without Alignment

*I'd like to schedule a meeting with you on _____ to
revisit _____ .*

**During our last meeting, we talked about how you often
operate too independently. You move ahead without consulting
with me, and you do not comply with our new business
principles.**

You agreed to:

> *more carefully align your statements and activities with the objectives defined in our last meeting.*
>
> *check with me before committing to _____ .*
>
> *involve me with decisions involving key customers.*
>
> *better inform me about _____ in your area.*
>
> *keep me up-to-date on _____ news relevant to our business.*
>
> *involve and acknowledge the people who are working with you.*

We also documented our discussion in this meeting note/e-mail.

Unfortunately you didn't live up to this agreement. Once again, you met with _____ and didn't include me. Also I noticed that you ignored _____ , and she is a key _____ .

We have discussed the negative impact your actions have on achieving our new goals. They:

> *bear the risks of uncoordinated efforts and wastefulness of resources.*
>
> *corroborate old practices we have painfully tried to eliminate.*
>
> *undermine the new spirit of collaboration I want to foster in our team.*
>
> *commit us to things we don't want to do anymore.*
>
> *demoralize your peers.*

What were your considerations when you _____ ?

Does this mean you are saying that _____ ?

I have a different point of view. I see _____ because _____ .

This has to change in the future. What are you going to do to assure me that you indeed can live up to our agreements?

Good. Let's capture that _____ .

Do you have any additional comments or questions?

Is there anything else you see that could prevent you from living up to our renewed agreement?

Let's schedule a meeting on _____ to check in.

Someone Not Following Decision-Making Rules
During our last meeting we talked about how important it is to adhere to our decision-making and collaboration guidelines, as captured in _____ .

You agreed to:

> *not spend money on noncritical initiatives.*
>
> *involve me when initiatives cost more than $_____ .*
>
> *approach your team to _____ .*
>
> *not jump rapidly to a conclusion but carefully evaluate all options.*
>
> *inform key stakeholders, as defined in _____ .*
>
> *speed up the decision-making process.*

As you remember we documented those points in _____ .

Unfortunately, you overstepped your boundaries again. Yesterday I received yet another e-mail from _____ informing me that you _____ .

We have discussed the negative impact this has on us all. It:

> *undermines my authority as the new leader.*
>
> *damages the reputation of our team.*

> *irritates me because I feel we are wasting time with these meetings.*
>
> *creates a need for micromanagement.*
>
> *undermines my trust in you.*
>
> *sets a bad example for the rest of the team.*
>
> *makes collaborating as a team unnecessarily difficult.*

Would you mind telling me what's preventing you from following our decision-making rules?

This means you are saying that _____ . Is this correct?

I look at this in another way because _____ .

Our decision-making rules are here to be respected. They are not meant to be bureaucratic nuisances. In fact, there are many good reasons for these rules, as we already have discussed. How can we prevent you from going "your own way" in the future? What will it take to make you accept and implement the guidelines?

Are you willing and able to do what we have just discussed?

Is there any additional support you need?

Is there anything else you see that could prevent you from fulfilling this?

Let's schedule a meeting on _____ to go through all your decisions and confirm compliance with our reconfirmed agreement.

Rallying Teams

Team Objectives

I'm looking forward to working with you all. Your backgrounds are impressive. You have important experiences, and I'm very much aware of your track records with the company. In order to succeed, we need to all be pulling in the same direction.

Our team/departmental/divisional/regional/functional goals are to:

> *consistently have a customer satisfaction of _____ .*
>
> *generate revenue of $_____ .*
>
> *reduce the cost of goods sold to _____ .*
>
> *increase website traffic by _____ percent.*
>
> *develop _____ (number of) new products by _____ .*
>
> *increase market share to _____ percent.*
>
> *increase compliance in our usage of _____ to _____ by _____ .*
>
> *grow by _____ percent by _____ .*

We each have our own role to play. Our individual goals support the larger team/department/division/region/function goals.

Can you tell me what your understanding of the team goals is?

Can you tell me what you understand your role and responsibility to be?

For top-performing teams, you might need to add:

Your track record indicates to me that you are a top-performing team! I am pleased to have the privilege of being your new leader and know that I have big shoes to fill. It will take our combined experience, skills, and commitment to continue on this steep trajectory. I'm committing to support you in any way I can and am looking forward to celebrating many more successes with our team.

For low-performing teams, you might need to add:

You have noticed that the new goals are challenging. Senior management has high expectations and is counting on us to create a greater overall contribution to the success of the company. It will take our combined experience, skills, and commitment to correct the (downward) trend. I'm committing to support you in any way I can and am expecting the same from you. We will all benefit from such a turnaround. Welcome to the first day of our new venture!

Teamwork Principles
While every individual plays a unique role, we can't forget that we also are all members of this team. We need to focus on how we add value to each other and the team results.

We depend on each other to do our parts. For example:

follow through on your commitments to each other. Be accountable to each other. We sink or swim together!

look out for each other and identify when another team member needs support.

tell each other what you need.

help others see how your area of responsibility complements and supports theirs.

Take ownership. Encourage each other's top performance and break down barriers by:

asking for feedback.

giving feedback.

sharing what has been working for you.

sharing information.

sharing ideas.

sharing observations.

sharing learning.

connecting each other to your respective networks.

Listen to each other and:

be certain you fully understand the needs and concerns of others before stating your case.

be respectful of opinions and approaches that differ from your own.

Give credit to each other's contributions.

Address conflicts directly as they occur. Escalate conflicts if they cannot be resolved.

I will evaluate your success based on how well you support others and the team.

Team Code of Conduct
How can we best:

share information?

make good decisions quickly?

assign tasks?

leverage each other's strength?

support each other in pursuing our interests?

exchange feedback in a timely and effective manner?

share what has been working for you?

share information?

share ideas?

share observations?

share learning?

connect to each other's network?

resolve conflicts?

Team Optimization

What has worked well in the past?

Please identify improvement options.

What's the one thing you most need from me and from each other to succeed?

Let's take some time to discuss each other's responsibilities and how they are interconnected.

I'd like each of you to put together a one-page summary of your key skills, knowledge, and experiences. Please also include any development interest you may have. Get it to me by _____ .

Chapter 5

Perfect Phrases for Communicating a New Organizational Strategy

Strategy change can be as challenging as a restructuring. While there isn't the high visibility and hoopla of a reorganization, employees face similar difficulties and experience levels of resistance and ambiguity but they are often more under the radar. Unfortunately, leaders often don't see this. Strategy changes are an opportunity for leaders to start anew and get employee commitment to success. Using these perfect phrases will help you hit the ground running.

Announcing Change

New Strategy Business Case
As you may have heard, we have decided to shift our strategy and modify our offerings, including _____ .

We are implementing this new strategy to:

> *better respond to our global customer base.*
> *take advantage of market opportunities.*
> *deal with changing economic conditions.*

emulate industry best practices.

better leverage our current/new technology.

better leverage our people.

save money.

Specifically, our objectives are to:

consistently have a customer satisfaction level of

_____ .

generate revenue of $_____ .

reduce costs of goods sold to $_____ .

increase website traffic by _____ .

develop _____ (number of) new products by

_____ .

increase market share to _____ .

increase compliance in the use of _____ to

_____ by _____ .

grow by _____ percent by _____ .

I know we have always been focused on _____ .
However, we feel like we have the capability to also meet the
needs of _____ . We made this decision because
_____ . This means we need to _____ .

If there is any impact on compensation, refer to the phrases for a new
compensation model in Chapter 2.

Getting Individual Buy-In
To make this happen, you will need to shift your priorities. For
example:

your short-term objectives will now be _____ .

your communication tasks need to include _____ .

you will be reporting to _____ .

Our budget is being reallocated as follows: _____ .

In this time of transition, the potential upside for you personally is that you will be able to:

> *leverage your expertise in a new area.*
>
> *expand the scope of your responsibility.*
>
> *rise to meet new challenges.*
>
> *work with new customers/industries.*

Responding to Questions

How Will This Impact My Future at the Company?
We will be looking for people who:

> *take initiative.*
>
> *apply creativity to solve these new problems.*
>
> *build on existing relationships.*
>
> *quickly build new relationships.*

Your talent and experience here will help to contribute to the change and grow your career with us.

This new strategy will open new opportunities for you, including _____ .

Why Didn't We Choose Another Strategy Instead?
We are implementing this new strategy to:

> *better respond to our global customer base.*
>
> *take advantage of market opportunities.*
>
> *deal with changing economic conditions.*
>
> *emulate industry best practices.*
>
> *better leverage our current/new technology.*

better leverage our people.

save money.

Based on what we expect to gain from the new strategy, we looked at several options, including _____.

This was the best option because _____.

Or

Given the situation, this was the only option because _____.

How Will This Change Impact Our Customers?
This new strategy opens new opportunities that our current customers will appreciate because we will soon be able to provide them with:

better response times.

more tailored services.

state-of-the-art technology.

more cost-effective solutions.

more individual attention.

Plus, we will be able to reach new customer segments, including _____.

This will be the basis for our future growth/success.

And/or

Serving our customers is at the core of our business and the lifeblood of our company. This change should not interfere with our dedication to providing our customers with the highest level of service.

If you encounter situations in which our change activities are interfering with our customer service, please speak to your manager for assistance.

We are in the process of working on relevant communications to our customers. We will be distributing a template to assist you by _____ .

For best practices, use questions to bring home your one-minute change message—the business case for change. Also, focus on clear short-term goals so that employees have direction and feel like they are making progress. Be prepared to answer questions such as

- Will there be layoffs? (See "Responding to Questions" in Chapter 2.)
- What were the main criteria for this decision?
- Who was involved in the decision?
- What is the competition doing?
- How much will this cost?
- How will we know if this is working?
- How long will this take?

Overcoming Fear

Someone Who Thinks the Strategy Won't Work
I understand that you believe the strategy won't work. Why do you think so?

I hear your points, and I understand what you are saying. However, I invite you to give it a chance. You know that we have set some very clear, measurable, timed objectives. As we have discussed, we have done our homework and the facts show _____ . Also, we have put _____ into place to support our success.

Let's convene at milestone one to reassess.

127

Creating Urgency

Keeping the Momentum
It is critical that we succeed in this new strategy so that we can:

> *stay number one in the market.*
>
> *become number one in the market by _____ .*
>
> *grow our business by _____ .*
>
> *diversify by adding _____ .*
>
> *expand into _____ .*
>
> *reduce our response time to _____ .*
>
> *improve our operational efficiencies.*
>
> *make _____ happy.*
>
> *comply with (new) legal requirements.*

By doing so, you/our team will have the opportunity to:

> *increase your salary/bonus.*
>
> *save your job.*
>
> *create more career and development opportunities for yourself/ our team.*

Addressing Power Struggles and Career Issues

How Does This New Strategy Help Your Career?
This is a critical strategy for the business. You'll gain a thorough understanding of it and as this strategy is implemented, you'll become a go-to person.

This strategy has high visibility. Senior executives will be watching.

You may be able to create new allegiances with key people in the company.

Implementing the strategy will give you the opportunity to develop new skills.

I know one of your career goals is _____ . This will help you reach that goal by _____ .

Clarifying Roles and Responsibilities

Let's do a brief review of your role and how it is impacted by the new strategy:

Your title will continue to be/will now be _____ to reflect _____ .

You will continue to report to/will now report to _____ because _____ .

Your key performance measures will continue to be/will now be _____ because _____ .

Your team members will continue to be/will now be _____ to allow you to take the new budget/ needed skill set/customers' needs into account.

Your main responsibilities will continue to be/will now be _____ . This means you will continue to/will stop/will start _____ .

What questions do you have?

What are you thoughts about this?

How does this compare with what you expected/what you were hoping for?

Communicating Individual Objectives

Clarifying What Is Expected
I'm referring back to our announcement and the communication introducing our new strategy. As you

remember, what we are trying to achieve with the new strategy is _____ .

Our team has a key contribution to bringing the new strategy to life.

In light of this new strategy, within the next _____ week(s), I would like you to:

contact your customers/suppliers/key contacts to introduce the new strategy.

have a staff meeting to review the strategy and answer any questions.

update goals with your direct reports, if necessary.

analyze the revised budget and its implications for the next quarter.

update relevant company marketing material.

create development plans for your people, if necessary.

plan a party to celebrate this milestone.

Empowering Employees

Individual Contributors
You have heard a lot about our new strategy and its business case. Now let's pull it off together! What you can do to help us succeed is:

Be certain you understand the strategy and its business case. Approach me with any questions you may have.

Once you know the new strategy in all its aspects, you will become your own boss within the parameter of company policies and the new strategy.

Focus on strategy execution. The best plans and ideas are useless if not implemented properly.

If you question or don't agree with a business decision, speak up! You may be right.

Learn about the key indicators (financial, operational, sales, etc.) we are using to track performance. Ask somebody in accounting, a peer, or your manager to help you.

Take a course in business finance, business acumen, or operations to help you make decisions in the larger context of our new strategy.

Keep me and other key stakeholders informed of your commitments and your progress in implementing the new strategy.

Develop/update your objectives in order to align with the new strategy. Make sure your key partners (direct reports, manager, other key business partners, etc.) are aware of those objectives.

Leaders
What you can do to help us succeed is:

Develop a local/regional/functional strategy that is in line with our global strategy.

Think about how our high-level, overall objectives apply to your business/division/region/department/team. Make sure you define individual objectives accordingly.

Review your resources and see how you can reallocate them to accommodate the priorities of the new strategy.

Involve your direct reports and delegate as much of the communication and implementation tasks to them as possible and within reason.

Regularly review your own and your team's/department's/division's/function's progress implementing the new strategy.

Refer to your team members' job descriptions. Make sure you understand their roles and responsibilities. Clarify their job descriptions, if necessary.

Involve all stakeholders as early as possible.

Keep me and other key stakeholders informed of commitments and project progress.

Keeping People Motivated

By Providing Clarity of Vision/Direction

The vision of the new strategy is to _____ .

Based on your responsibilities, your number one priority is _____ .

The most important success criteria is _____ .

Your key performance measure is _____ .

Don't worry about _____ . We have _____ taking care of it now.

We have already achieved major milestones. But now is not a time to rest on our laurels. There are major implementation challenges still to be overcome. I need you to particularly focus on _____ .

By Relationship-Building and Team-Building

How are things going?

Thank you! This will bring us a long way in implementing our new strategy.

I'm calling you instead of sending an e-mail to discuss _____ , since this is the first time we are dealing with this issue.

Can I offer you _____?

Did you know _____ is available? It has helped me greatly.

Let's have lunch together.

I'd like to recognize our collective effort by all going out for _____ together.

I'm very confident we'll get this done. We have implemented _____ before, which was at least as complex and tricky—if not more.

This is a team effort. We have assembled the best talent to implement the new strategy.

By Recognizing and Celebrating Progress
These are examples of where the implementation of the new strategy is going well: _____ .

Our new strategy has already received recognition and acclaim in the industry. This confirms that we are on the right track!

At _____ conference last week, I heard that our competition is becoming very nervous.

Let's go to _____ and celebrate _____ .

I couldn't have done it without your engagement. I'm glad you are on our team!

You are a role model to our team. I am particularly impressed with the speed with which you have started implementing our new strategy.

This _____ is a terrific sign of progress. The transition to the new strategy is moving along very well.

By Showing Trust and Support

I'm behind you on that decision!

Don't hesitate to approach me if you have a question or an issue.

You can call me at any time.

I'll take care of that for you.

This is a challenge, but you can do it because _____ .

I know you have never done that before, but I'm confident you'll succeed because _____ .

There is no one I trust more than you to do this because _____ .

I like your input! Let's try it.

I would never have thought of that, but I love your suggestion. Let's try it.

It's less important to me how you do it. I just would like to get _____ *(result).*

Yes, you did make a mistake. Only people who do nothing don't make mistakes! Strategy implementation requires a level of risk-taking and experimenting. Thanks for trying!

By Providing Learning Opportunities

Knowing _____ *is key to the success of our implementing the new strategy. Is there any training/coaching/ mentoring that would prepare you even better for those tasks?*

I'm giving you this assignment because I think it will prepare you for _____ , *which will be key to our new strategy.*

I am counting on you for the long term, which is why I suggest you take _____ training.

We all recognize that we didn't succeed with _____. But it was worth trying. Let's see what we learned from it.

Let's focus on what's working and how we can leverage that for the new environment.

By Making Decisions Expeditiously

We want to make a decision on _____ now! This will allow us to keep the implementation on schedule.

I'm calling _____ and will get back to you with an answer/a decision by tomorrow.

Let's have a meeting this afternoon to decide on _____ so we can move forward.

This issue will be taken care of by tomorrow. I'm not delaying its resolution!

If you have doubts, refer back to the strategy document, which includes both the business case and the implementation plan. Use your judgment. Only refer back to me/escalate if _____.

By Including and Involving People

Since this new _____ will impact you, I want to consult with you before I decide. What do you think?

You know most about _____. I trust your judgment. Tell me how we should proceed.

I don't have the answer. Please discuss this with _____. The two of you will decide together.

By Relieving Stress and Having Fun
We are providing food for our strategy lunch sessions every _____ .

Let's create new strategy artifacts around sports themes and then actively use them. What about:

> *golf balls for persistence?*
>
> *hiking binoculars for observing and forecasting?*
>
> *soccer balls for collaboration and teamwork?*
>
> *bike helmets for safety?*
>
> *Swiss army knives for having a tool for any situation?*
>
> *basketballs for agility and speed?*

Take note of what is on your mind and discuss your thoughts with somebody you trust.

Find the humor in the challenges you're having. It's a good way to relieve stress.

Coaching Around Emotions

Someone Who Says He/She Is on Board but Doesn't Take Initiative
Adjusting to our new strategy and switching gears has certainly been a challenge for most of us. It seems like you are struggling.

I hear you saying you support the new strategy. However, what I have noticed is that you haven't implemented it into the way you do your daily business.

Your lack of support is resulting in negative consequences. You are:

> *losing precious time/delaying the implementation.*
>
> *losing credibility.*
>
> *demotivating your peers.*

putting my objectives at risk with my manager.

confusing those who report to you.

*unnecessarily creating animosity within the rest of the
    organization.*

*unnecessarily creating resistance within the rest of the
    organization.*

eroding the morale of your coworkers.

What are your thoughts at this point?

*So we agree that going forward you will _____ and
I will _____ .*

Someone Who Complains About Not Having Enough People/Technology/Budget to Succeed

*I hear you saying that our limited resources may conflict with
our ability to implement the strategy.*

Let's take a few minutes and examine this in detail.

*Given that we can't expand our budget, are not authorized to
hire more employees, and have to live with the technology as it
stands, how can we succeed within our constraints?*

*You are right: We could use more people/budget/technology.
We don't have it. However, doing nothing is not an option! What
do you suggest?*

*Are there any resources that can be allocated from other areas/
projects?*

Someone Who Believes the Change Is Incompatible with the Company Culture

*This is different than anything we have ever done before, and it
certainly takes courage to take such a bold approach. We all have
our ambivalence about the strategy, and I know you do, too.*

Still, there are good reasons for choosing this strategy, including _____ .

I notice that you don't miss an opportunity to express your discontent with this strategy. For example, _____ .

What are your thoughts?

Your lack of support is resulting in negative consequences. You are:

> *delaying our progress.*
>
> *demotivating your peers.*
>
> *putting my objectives at risk with my manager.*
>
> *confusing those who report to you.*
>
> *unnecessarily creating animosity within the rest of the organization.*
>
> *unnecessarily creating resistance within the rest of the organization.*
>
> *eroding the morale of your coworkers.*
>
> *reducing the responsiveness and quality of our customer service.*

We need to make this work within the constraints we have. How can we?

I am counting on you to follow through with these ideas and make this strategy a success.

Someone Who Says the Change Is Not Going Far Enough
You are right. More could be done. While we are implementing this new strategy, we are very carefully monitoring our success. This will allow us to fine-tune as we go. What ideas do you have to increase our success in the future?

What I have captured is _____. Does this accurately summarize your ideas? Thank you for your input.

In the meantime please be patient and follow our step-by-step approach. Rome wasn't built in a day. Can you live with that?

Coaching for Skills

New Skills
This new strategy will shift the parameters of your job. Accordingly, there are new skills you should acquire/refresh.

Do you have any thoughts about what new skills you will need in order to succeed within this new strategy?

You might want to consider what skills you will need in order to reach your objectives and rise to a higher level of competence. From there, we could come up with a development plan.

Because the new strategy is a significant departure from what we have done before and because a thorough understanding of the strategy, its motives, and its impact are key to your future success in the company, I invite you to:

> *familiarize yourself with our new strategy documents/website/ resources. If you come across any piece of information that you are not clear about, ask me questions.*

> *talk to each other about what we must do to see the strategy through.*

> *stay close to our customers, our key employee groups, and our critical suppliers in order to ensure we implement the strategy in the most effective way possible.*

> *study reports and statistics about our new markets.*

> *subscribe to newsletters and publications relevant to our new strategy.*

be aware of other factors (governmental, environmental, economic, etc.) that drive or impact strategic decisions.

familiarize yourself with our competitive landscape.

Google your industry, your competition, and your customers to understand what drives business in our sector.

read business publications and journals that are relevant to our new markets.

attend industry conferences.

Great, so we agreed that you _____.

Skill Gaps

I noticed that you are struggling to maintain the higher level of quality/output/accuracy/speed that our new strategy requires. For example, I noticed that _____, whereas the expectation is that you _____.

What:

do you think you are lacking?

do you think we can do to help you?

would best support you?

training do you think would help?

is interfering?

Who:

in your team/department/company could coach you on that?

has excelled in this area before you can turn to as an example?

is a thought leader/consultant in this area you can turn to as an example?

Let's discuss ideas of how we could address these issues.

Great, so we agreed that you _____.

Coaching for Flexibility and Adaptability

Offering Direction and Support

Implementing new strategies is a big job. We are all contributing to the success of the new strategy. Specifically we need you to:

> *respond flexibly to our new strategic direction.*
>
> *be willing to reprioritize your workload.*
>
> *be open to new ways of working.*
>
> *help/support others in implementing the new strategy.*
>
> *live with the ambiguity that this change brings.*

This is a lot of stuff, isn't it? Let me ask you:

> *Can you think of times when you were in similar situations? What did you do to adapt?*
>
> *How are you coping with the stress that comes with implementing the new strategy?*
>
> *How are you finding time to balance business and the rest of your life?*
>
> *Whom do you turn to for advice and support?*
>
> *How do you normally adapt to change?*
>
> *Is there anything I can do to help you be more adaptable?*

Here are some pieces of advice and tips on how to navigate this strategic transformation:

> *Expect change. Let go of your preconceived notions of how business is done here.*
>
> *Apply proactive thinking. Anticipate the market's future needs and identify potential internal developments.*
>
> *Identify people you trust whom you can go to if you're not sure or worried.*

Speak up if you are unclear about your level of responsibility or accountability.

Embrace diversity. Stay mentally flexible and open to new ideas.

Be willing to change your approach—as long as it doesn't compromise your or our company's values.

Read books and articles on innovative and creative thinking.

When striving for the "best" solution, be sure you're also being reasonable.

Maintain a network of colleagues from outside our company to stay abreast of best practices.

Addressing Performance Problems

Someone Who Is Not Following the Principles of the New Strategy

I'd like to schedule a meeting with you on _____ to revisit _____ .

During our last meeting, we discussed the obstacles that have been preventing you from following the principles of our new strategy. We also devised an approach to overcoming these obstacles. You agreed to:

read the marketing documentation associated with the new strategy and put forth any questions you may have.

draw up a plan that details what your team will do to best support the new strategy.

revise all communication materials so that they align with our new strategy.

rally your team behind the new strategy through proactive and comprehensive communication with your direct reports, _____ (peer), and _____ (peer).

We documented our discussion in the available meeting notes.

Unfortunately, I have not seen enough progress in your efforts to follow the principles of the new strategy. Namely, your statements at _____ barely mentioned the new strategy. Also your proposed _____ budget didn't sufficiently reflect the new course.

At our last meeting, we discussed the negative impact your failure to follow the principles of the new strategy has had on the company's ability to effectively implement the strategy. Among other concerns, it:

> *slows down the implementation process.*
>
> *spreads conflicting messages within our organization as well as to our customers.*
>
> *creates unnecessary tension.*
>
> *wastes resources.*
>
> *harms our reputation, both as individuals and as members of a larger team.*
>
> *prevents organizational learning.*

Would you mind explaining the challenges you have encountered with appropriately implementing the new strategy?

If I hear you right, you are saying that _____ .

I see this differently. What I see is _____ because _____ .

In order for the new strategy to be executed smoothly, you will have to accept and live by the strategy principles we captured at our last meeting. Let's discuss how we can ensure that you indeed can live up to these principles.

I'm capturing your updated action planning as _____ .
Do you agree?

Are you willing to recommit to our agreement?

Are you willing and able to execute all the actions we have
discussed and captured?

Is there any additional support I can provide?

Is there any aspect of following the principles of the new
strategy that we have overlooked?

Thank you! Let's schedule a meeting on _____ to
check in and monitor your progress.

Someone Who Is Promoting Bad News About the New Strategy

During our last meeting we talked about your negativity and
how you often focus on the deficiencies and drawbacks of
the new strategy instead of looking at how it has helped us
progress as an organization and has opened up countless new
opportunities.

You agreed to:

> *actively manage a list of new opportunities that have arisen as*
> *a result of the new strategy.*
>
> *meet with _____ twice every month to discuss the*
> *key accomplishments of the strategy for that time period*
> *and create new strategy success stories.*
>
> *escalate anything that seems to be going wrong with the*
> *strategy directly to me and approach me to discuss.*
>
> *frequently recognize team members for a job well done.*
>
> *revisit the business case and actively communicate the what*
> *and the why of the new strategy.*

identify all the ways in which successful implementation of the new strategy will help your region/department/team and forward the list to me by _____ .

We documented the discussion we had at this meeting in this note/e-mail.

Let's go through the list and see which strategy-related tasks you have completed.

As you just confirmed, there are too many items on the list that you have yet to complete.

The last time we spoke, we detailed how your behavior is negatively impacting collaboration within our organization and the team's implementation of the new strategy. We mentioned, for example, that it:

unnecessarily confuses the direction of the new strategy.

causes negative rumors to be spread about the new strategy.

spoils the confidence of the team/department/region/company regarding the successful implementation of this strategy.

negatively impacts the morale of your direct reports.

creates anxiety and ambiguity, which are toxic to new initiatives.

further complicates communication and creates unnecessary noise in the system.

Can you tell me why so many of the action items on our previously agreed-upon list have not yet been implemented?

What I'm hearing is that _____ .

I see this differently because _____ .

The action plan needs to be honored in the future. Let's discuss how we can ensure that you can get back on track and implement the action plan.

Do you agree?

Are you willing to recommit to this action plan?

Are you willing and able to execute all the actions we have discussed and captured?

Is there any additional support I can provide?

Is there anything else we should know about that could prevent you from fulfilling these expectations?

Let's schedule a meeting on _____ to check in on your progress.

Rallying Teams

Personal Goals
I am proud of our team and its members and appreciate your individual and collective experience and track records. This new strategy presents an opportunity for us to shine. After all, we play an important role in ensuring its success. There is a lot we can gain from the success of the new strategy, such as:

> *profit and rewards.*
> *visibility.*
> *career opportunities.*
> *exposure to cutting-edge experiences/technologies/practices.*
> *learning.*
> *travel.*
> *expanded networking opportunities with our strategy collaborators.*

Team Objectives
To reiterate, our updated goals and priorities are to:

consistently satisfy our customers.

generate revenue of $_____ .

reduce cost of goods sold to _____ .

increase website traffic by _____ percent.

develop _____ (number of) new products
by _____ .

increase market share to _____ percent.

increase compliance in our usage of _____ to
_____ by _____ .

grow by _____ percent by _____ .

Team Code of Conduct
Given this new challenge, how can we continue to best:

share information?

make good decisions quickly?

assign tasks?

leverage each other's strength?

support each other in pursuing our interests?

exchange feedback in a timely and effective manner?

share what has been working?

share information?

share ideas?

share observations?

share learning?

connect to each other's networks?

resolve conflicts?

Team Optimization

What do you need from the team in order to successfully implement this new strategy?

Let's take some time to discuss each other's modified responsibilities and how they interrelate.

What should we change about the way we are working regarding:

> *systems and technology?*
>
> *processes?*
>
> *attitudes?*

Chapter 6

Perfect Phrases for Handling Resistance

Everyone resists change. It is normal. The problem occurs when this normal resistance becomes stubborn and inflexible. We call this *persistent resistance*. How can you tell the difference? Normal resistance is the natural reaction everyone has at first to something imposed on them. They ask questions and challenge it. They act a bit strange for a while. If you take time to talk with them and discuss their point of view, this will pass. Next comes what we call *business resistance*. These are real business questions/issues that emerge during a change that must be addressed. How will I be measured in my new job? How will I get the skills I need to succeed in the new environment? Again, if you address these head-on, people will move past them. Persistent resistance is what happens to some people, despite your best efforts to handle the previous types of resistance. They continue to complain about, avoid, and undermine the change.

In addition to reading this chapter, we assume you have been coaching your employees to overcome their resistance by supplying ample information, taking the time to listen to their concerns, addressing real business issues with adequate answers and solutions, making suggestions for how to move forward, and supporting their successes in general. We also assume that, if you are still reading, your efforts have not worked. The scenarios presented here are what we have found to be the most common persisting resistance issues and the best approaches to overcome them.

Structuring Your Phrases

What follows are four elements of the perfect phrases that will help you come out on top when speaking with persistently resistant employees.

1. **Empathize.** Resistance at its core is emotional. Before charging into an attack to try to challenge the employees' point of view, it is critical to establish an emotional connection and let them know you understand where they are coming from. This is done through statements such as "I can see what you mean" or "That makes perfect sense. I have felt that way in other situations."

2. **Level.** Now that they know you are listening to them, it is time to shock them into reality. They need to hear the truth about how they are coming across. You need to honestly disclose what you see them doing and how it is impacting the people and project. For example, "You continue to look for a perfect solution. There is none. This is slowing us down and preventing us from making progress on a practical one."

3. **Listen.** Once you've shared your point of view, you can either just pause or ask an open-ended question such as "What do you think about this?" to get them back into the conversation. They need one last chance to say, "I see what you mean. I need your help to stop."

4. **Take a stand.** The last step is to let the employees know what the consequences will be if they don't give you their

commitment to joining the change. This commitment can be anything that is appropriate to your organization, including reassignment, a negative report on their performance review, less money, and the option of termination (but only if you have tried everything else before, you have written documentation, and you have consulted with a trusted and competent individual in your company—often your manager and/or your Human Resources representative).

While we use these four elements in each phrase in this chapter, we present them using a number of different styles. We suggest you read through several phrases before choosing your approach, even if the content is not relevant. This will help you find a style that fits you and your situation.

New Structure

Someone Who Says He/She Is on Board but Doesn't Take Initiative

I have heard you say you are on board with and support the new structural changes, but when it comes to the implementation of the new structure, I have not seen any proof of your commitment. I expected you to:

> *communicate with your team.*
>
> *draft new job descriptions for your team members.*
>
> *create a package that communicates the structural changes to our stakeholders.*
>
> *leverage your influence as an ambassador for this change.*

Your lack of support is resulting in negative consequences. You are:

> *losing precious time/delaying the implementation of dependent tasks.*

losing credibility.

demotivating your peers.

putting my objectives at risk with my manager.

confusing those who report to you.

unnecessarily creating animosity within the rest of the organization.

unnecessarily creating resistance within the rest of the organization

eroding the morale of your coworkers.

I need you on board. If you are not able to, then _____.

Someone Who Complains About Not Having Enough People/Technology/Budget to Succeed

We spoke about this, and I have tried to help you understand our limited resources as well as the priorities we have set. A key leadership/managerial skill is getting the most out of what you have to work with. However, it sounds like you are still frustrated with the changes.

You know, _____ (name), I have to level with you. We have been around this topic _____ times. I hear what you're saying and have tried to work with you on this.

Your negativity is beginning to affect others. If you can't live with the new parameters of your position, then I have no choice but to look at different options/look for different positions for you/write you up.

Someone Who Is Overwhelmed

I hear you and understand your feelings. I too have been faced with challenging situations that have caused me to feel overwhelmed.

You are right; there is a lot to do and work can seem overwhelming at times.

Are there any new work-related stressors that have arisen since our last conversation?

We have had this conversation a few times already. I have tried to help you manage your workload, set priorities, and plan a step-by-step approach to fulfilling the responsibilities of your job. It seems to me as if you cannot do the job or don't want to do it. This may sound harsh, but I am asking you directly: Do you really want to make this work?

We may need to look for another position for you and find someone better suited to this one.

Someone Who Is Slowing Progress with Too Many Questions and Seems Inflexible

I know that we don't have all the information/all the answers to every single question that may arise.

I appreciate how thoroughly you think your decisions through before making them. You obviously understand that we need to make the best decisions possible as we move forward. However, sometimes we have to move forward before we know all the potential ramifications that may arise from our actions/ decisions. To wait would be too risky/too costly/not an option.

We have made every effort to determine the outcome of this decision. However, now we are relying on the ingenuity, experience, and wisdom of our team to start the implementation process and hammer out the remaining details.

Your desire to know all the possible outcomes of a decision before making it sometimes gets in the way of our progress. We have to move ahead with "the good" and build the perfect later.

I'll ask you one last time, "What do you need to move forward more quickly?"

The next time this happens, we will have to _____ .

Someone Whose Role Has Changed but Keeps Doing Former Tasks

I have observed that you are continuing to do your old job as if nothing has changed, even though we have discussed the related details of your new position and have established a step-by-step transition plan. Why is this happening?

Your behavior is having a huge impact! Nobody can move ahead, and we can't give the new organization a chance if you aren't willing to change. Are you up for this new job?

I am referring back to the job profile we discussed. Please implement it. I will reassess how you are progressing with the transition into your new position in _____ days. If you are not demonstrating clear progress by that date, I will assume your new position is not an ideal fit. At that point in time, I suggest we discuss alternative jobs for you.

Someone Who Believes the Change Is Incompatible with the Company Culture

As we have discussed, we chose a global solution. We need you to tailor this global standard to your area/function/region.

Your focus and emphasis on culture/fit has begun to look like an excuse to not take action.

We need to make this new structure work. Do you think you are able to do it?

If that is your final answer, we need to _____ .

Someone Overly Concerned with Status and Less Concerned with the Change

I know that your title change has been a struggle for you. However, after all of our discussions, why do you still refuse to:

> *change your e-mail signature to reflect your new title?*
>
> *use your new business cards?*
>
> *change your voice mail message to reflect your new title?*
>
> *introduce yourself to customers with your new title?*
>
> *accept your new title?*
>
> *try out your new title, instead of insisting that it is inconsistent with your job responsibilities?*

I do not see enough progress from you in accepting the new dynamics of our company. What's more, your commitment to this company seems contingent upon your happiness with your job title.

I need to be very frank: I'm looking for people who fully support our new vision, even if it negatively affects them in the short term. Are you willing to join us and stand fully behind the change?

I don't want to be overly harsh. I appreciate everything you have done for me and for the company. However, I don't want to leave any doubt in your mind. If you are not able to overcome your disappointment and fully support the new direction of the company, you will need to look for employment elsewhere. Please think it over and get back to me by _____ .

Someone Who Says the Change Is Not Going Far Enough

You are right. More could be done. However, as was mentioned in our previous conversation, the perfect is the enemy of the good. We have to be pragmatic and start somewhere.

It seems to me that you are hiding behind a perfectionist view of how you think we should be progressing. Do you understand why I have this impression?

I need to have a commitment from you. Are you willing to support our new structure as it is?

Someone Constantly Arguing with Other People
Although we have spoken about this matter before, you still are frequently getting into arguments with _____ .

On _____ (date), I clearly communicated to you that your arguments with _____ were unacceptable. You agreed on _____ to cease arguing with _____ , yet last _____ you started yet another argument.

Your behavior is negatively impacting morale/reducing productivity/creating animosity between your team and an important business partner. Additionally, people from both within and outside the company have approached me about your behavior.

Can you please explain what's happening?

These arguments need to stop. I'll be assigning you to this coach/mentor/Human Resources representative, who will help you work through this problem. I am happy to help in any way I can to turn your relationship with _____ around. Your contributions to our business have been significant, and our success is dependent upon your ability to work with key partners like _____ across the company.

Someone Who Is Bored and Disengaged

We spoke about this matter before, but, unfortunately, I have not seen any change in your behavior and attitudes.

This change was designed to reinvent our company. We are trying to achieve something new/better/faster. We need you to help us build our future, but you remain disengaged from your work/the company. You are not participating or asking questions. It seems like you quit and stayed.

You could be a key contributor to this change, yet your lack of engagement is preventing you from doing so.

Your lack of engagement must be corrected. Please confirm that you are willing to fully engage in your work/the company again and inform me of how you intend to adjust your behavior.

Should you not be interested in engaging in your work/the company anymore, I suggest we discuss other options. How would you like to proceed?

New Project

Someone Who Says He/She Is on Board but Doesn't Take Initiative

I understand you have mixed feelings about your new assignment. We have spoken about your concerns before.

I continue to hear you say that you want to be on this project. However, I have noticed that you have made no progress with any of your project assignments. Your lack of initiative is resulting in negative consequences. You are:

> *losing precious time/delaying the implementation of dependent tasks.*
> *losing credibility.*

demotivating the project team.

putting my objectives at risk with my manager.

What's going on?

If you do not make any progress by _____ , I will have no choice but to take you off the project. I assume you are aware that if this were to happen, it would not reflect favorably on you.

Someone Who Complains About Not Having Enough People/Technology/Budget to Succeed

It seems like you are still frustrated with your assignment to the project.

I have to level with you. We have been around this topic _____ times. I hear what you're saying and have tried to work with you on this.

Your negativity is beginning to affect others. If you can't live with your assignment, I will have no choice but to take you off the project. I assume you are aware that if this were to happen, it would not reflect favorably upon you.

Someone Who Is Overwhelmed

I hear you and understand your feelings. I too have been faced with challenging situations that have caused me to feel overwhelmed.

We have had this conversation a few times already. I have tried to help you manage your workload, set priorities, and plan a step-by-step approach to fulfilling the responsibilities of your job. It seems to me as if you cannot do the job or don't want to do it. This may sound harsh, but I am asking you directly: Do you really want to make this work?

*We need someone on this project who can get it done,
so unless you figure this out, I have no other choice but
to _____ .*

Someone Constantly Opposing Project Methodology and Policies

*I understand that you are struggling to adjust to the new
requirements and processes of this project because you are
more familiar with other methodologies. However, even though
you have been given extensive training and ample time to
adjust to the new methodologies and policies, you continue to
apply your own rules and approaches to this project.*

What do we need to do to overcome this once and for all?

*I heard you, but I need your commitment. If you refuse to
change your behavior, I will have no choice but to:*

> *reassign you to another task.*
>
> *take you off the project.*
>
> *talk to your boss.*
>
> *write you up.*

*We are relying on your ingenuity/experience/professionalism to
bring this project to a successful completion.*

New Leader

Someone Who Says He/She Is on Board but Doesn't Take Initiative

*We met _____ , at which point in time you told me
that you support me. However, your actions do not reflect your
words. I haven't noticed any change in your behavior.*

159

Your lack of support is resulting in negative consequences. You are:

> *losing precious time/delaying the implementation of dependent tasks.*
>
> *losing credibility.*
>
> *demotivating your peers.*
>
> *putting my objectives at risk with my manager.*
>
> *confusing those who report to you.*
>
> *unnecessarily creating animosity within the rest of the organization.*
>
> *unnecessarily creating resistance within the rest of the organization.*
>
> *eroding the morale of your coworkers.*
>
> *reducing the responsiveness and quality of our customer service.*

I expected you to:

> *clearly communicate our decisions with your team.*
>
> *walk the talk.*
>
> *live up to our values and principles.*
>
> *leverage your influence as an ambassador for our new initiatives.*

If you are not willing to get behind me, I will need to _____. Can I get your support and commitment?

Someone Who Believes the Change Is Incompatible with the Company Culture
Even though we take the time to discuss the pros and cons of new ideas and approaches before determining whether or not to proceed with them, you still are not supporting our final decisions.

Your lack of support is unacceptable. I need you to confirm that you are willing to fully engage in our decision-making process and inform me of how you intend to adjust your behavior.

Should you not be interested in engaging in our decision-making process, I suggest we discuss other options. How would you like to proceed?

New Strategy

Someone Who Says He/She Is on Board but Doesn't Take Initiative

I hear you saying that you support the new strategy. However, I have noticed that you still haven't implemented it into the way you conduct your daily business.

Your lack of support is resulting in negative consequences. You are:

> *losing credibility.*
>
> *demotivating your peers.*
>
> *putting my objectives at risk with my manager.*
>
> *confusing those who report to you.*
>
> *unnecessarily creating animosity within the rest of the organization.*
>
> *unnecessarily creating resistance within the rest of the organization.*
>
> *eroding the morale of your coworkers.*
>
> *reducing the responsiveness and quality of our customer service.*

We need your full support in order for the strategy to succeed. Can I get your full commitment? If you can't commit to the strategy, we will need to look for new options for you. Consider how committed you are to the new strategy and communicate your answer to me tomorrow.

Someone Who Complains About Not Having Enough People/Technology/Budget to Succeed
It sounds like you are still frustrated with the resource limitations.

We have discussed your frustrations multiple times. I have tried to work through them with you.

Our strategy is essential to who we are and where we are going as a company/organization. If you cannot find a way to support our plans, you will have to find a new future elsewhere.

I'm willing to support your decision, no matter what you decide. Let's schedule another meeting in a day or two to discuss which path you would like to choose.

Someone Who Believes the Change Is Incompatible with the Company Culture
I have to assume you are giving it your best. However, I continue to observe that you don't miss an opportunity to express your discontent with this strategy.

I need you to move past the "not-invented-here" thinking and make this work in your area. Your contributions and leadership make a huge difference to the company, and we need your support to make this new strategy work. Are you willing to make this work? By when can I get your commitment?

Someone Who Says the Change Is Not Going Far Enough

You are right. More could be done. However, as we already have discussed, the perfect is the enemy of the good. We have to be pragmatic and start somewhere.

It seems to me that you are hiding behind a perfectionist view of how you think we should be progressing. I need your commitment. Are you able to support the new strategy as it is?

About the Authors

Over the past twenty years, Lawrence Polsky and Antoine Gerschel have lived strategy implementation challenges in many shapes and forms, with firsthand experience in the United States, Europe, and Asia. They have more than fifteen years of experience developing award-winning programs that improve business communication and leadership within global, multicultural settings.

Polsky is a business-minded learning and development specialist with the ability to quickly analyze business situations and design learning scenarios and events to energize audiences of all sizes and makeup. He is an entrepreneur who, after a career in the financial services, health care, and consumer-electronics industries, launched and managed two businesses. He has also built a gourmet organic food-service business and an organization-development and training business.

He is an expert in organization development and learning, having taught more than 4,300 professionals around the world. He is also a pioneer in the business application of Daniel Goleman's emotional intelligence research, which was based on postgraduate work at the Institute of Human Development and completed under the direction of Dr. Wilson Tilley. In addition, Polsky has a master's in organization development with NTL Institute, the nation's leading program on experiential learning.

An extraordinary executive coach, Gerschel approaches human problems with a powerful mix of business perspective and sensitivity to human factors. His senior management experience enables him to consult, coach, and train leaders with a practical business approach. His experience includes serving as a COO of a 100-person, $17 million multimedia learning company in Europe and holding the position of director of global leadership development and e-learning for Aventis Pharmaceutical. He has firsthand experience working around the globe and is fluent in many languages, including English, German, French, and Spanish.

The authors are founding partners at PeopleNRG, Inc. (peoplenrg .com), in Princeton, New Jersey. Through speeches, workshops, and coaching assignments, they inspire leaders around the world to propel their teams, divisions, or companies in new directions.

PeopleNRG offerings include

- Keynotes
- Executive coaching
- Workshops and webinars
- Change-management programs
- Team-building events
- Leadership-development programs
- Leader and team assessments
- Engagement metrics

Exclusive to readers of this book, the authors will provide special reduced pricing for the companion online and in-person programs "Change Communication Lab," "Change Communication Clinic," and "Change Communication Coaching." For more information, contact them at (609) 333-0653 or info@peoplenrg.com.

The Right Phrase for Every Situation...Every Time

Perfect Phrases for Building Strong Teams
Perfect Phrases for Business Letters
Perfect Phrases for Business Proposals and Business Plans
Perfect Phrases for Business School Acceptance
Perfect Phrases for College Application Essays
Perfect Phrases for Cover Letters
Perfect Phrases for Customer Service
Perfect Phrases for Dealing with Difficult People
Perfect Phrases for Dealing with Difficult Situations at Work
Perfect Phrases for Documenting Employee Performance Problems
Perfect Phrases for Executive Presentations
Perfect Phrases for Landlords and Property Managers
Perfect Phrases for Law School Acceptance
Perfect Phrases for Lead Generation
Perfect Phrases for Managers and Supervisors
Perfect Phrases for Managing Your Small Business
Perfect Phrases for Medical School Acceptance
Perfect Phrases for Meetings
Perfect Phrases for Motivating and Rewarding Employees
Perfect Phrases for Negotiating Salary & Job Offers
Perfect Phrases for Perfect Hiring
Perfect Phrases for the Perfect Interview
Perfect Phrases for Performance Reviews
Perfect Phrases for Real Estate Agents & Brokers
Perfect Phrases for Resumes
Perfect Phrases for Sales and Marketing Copy
Perfect Phrases for the Sales Call
Perfect Phrases for Setting Performance Goals
Perfect Phrases for Small Business Owners
Perfect Phrases for the TOEFL Speaking and Writing Sections
Perfect Phrases for Writing Grant Proposals
Perfect Phrases in American Sign Language for Beginners
Perfect Phrases in French for Confident Travel
Perfect Phrases in German for Confident Travel
Perfect Phrases in Italian for Confident Travel
Perfect Phrases in Spanish for Confident Travel to Mexico
Perfect Phrases in Spanish for Construction
Perfect Phrases in Spanish for Gardening and Landscaping
Perfect Phrases in Spanish for Household Maintenance and Child Care
Perfect Phrases in Spanish for Restaurant and Hotel Industries

Visit mhprofessional.com/perfectphrases for a complete product listing.

Learn more. Do more.